Marketing Across Cultures in Asia

Richard R. Gesteland & Georg F. Seyk

Marketing
Across Cultures in Asia

Copenhagen Business School Press

Marketing Across Cultures in Asia

© *Copenhagen Business School Press*, 2002
Cover design: Kontrapunkt
Set in Plantin and printed by Narayana Press, Gylling

Printed in Denmark
1.edition 2002

ISBN 87-630-0094-6

Distribution:

Scandinavia
Djoef/DBK, Siljangade 2-8, P.O. Box 1731
DK-2300 Copenhagen S, Denmark
phone: +45 3269 7788, fax: +45 3269 7789

North America
Copenhagen Business School Press
Books International Inc.
P.O. Box 605
Hendon, VA 20172-0605, USA
phone: +1 703 661 1500, fax: +1 703 661 1501

Rest of the World
Marston Book Services, P.O. Box 269
Abingdon, Oxfordshire, OX14 4YN, UK
phone: +44 (0) 1235 465500, fax: +44 (0) 1235 465555
E-mail Direct Customers: direct.order@marston.co.uk
E-mail Booksellers: trade.order@marston.co.uk

Contents

About the Authors

George F. Seyk has worked as Division Manager of International Marketing and Sales for Littelfuse Inc. as well as Country Manager for Littelfuse K. K. Japan and Managing Director of Littelfuse-Triad Korea. Littelfuse is a leading global manufacturer of circuit protection devices that has seen double-digit growth in Asia.

George has also held international and domestic sales positions with the Cherry Corporation, ITW, and IBM. He has over 18 years of experience in establishing and managing Asian sales channels.

Outside of Asia, Mr. Seyk has extensive experience working with US, European, and Latin American operations. His efforts in the area of distribution development won him recognition from the Harvard Business Review.

George has an MA in Sociology and a BA in Psychology, and did postgraduate study in business. He lectures at the University of Wisconsin and has been a frequent speaker at industry and trade associations.

Richard R. Gesteland is a consultant, author and seminar leader conducting training programs for clients around the world in Managing, Marketing, Negotiating and Sourcing Across Cultures.

His international management career from 1963 to 1993 with two U.S. companies included eight expatriate assignments in six countries: Germany (twice), Austria, Italy, Brazil, India (twice) and Singapore. He was Regional Director, South and Southeast Asia and Vice President for Europe-Mideast-Africa with Sears Roebuck's global sourcing subsidiary. In 1994 he founded the Global Management consultancy in the U.S.

Richard has conducted seminars at the International Trade Institute of Singapore since 1990, the University of Wisconsin Management Institute and the Copenhagen Business School since 1994, Fachhochschule Reutlingen (Germany) since 1996, the Gdansk (Poland) Management Training Foundation since 1998, and the Stockholm School of Economics since 2000.

His articles on international business issues have appeared in the Asian Wall Street Journal, the UN International Trade Forum, Chief Executive Asia and many other publications. Richard's book *Cross-Cultural Business Behavior* (Copenhagen Business School Press: 1996, 1999) has been translated into German, Lithuanian and Polish; an English-language edition appeared in India in 2000. In 2000 he co-authored a textbook for Danish business colleges: *The Global Manager At Work* (Systime; Aarhus, Denmark).

Foreword

Doing business in Asia is challenging. The scope of its markets is daunting; the cultural differences among its business people extreme. But when handled correctly, those factors are also what make doing business in Asia a wonderful adventure. And that is what this book is about.

I owe my success to a large number of people, but particularly to my wife Liane. I dedicate this book to her; she is a testimony to all who support their spouses in such a demanding job.

I also want to thank Linda Gorchels who introduced me to Richard and made this book possible. She inspired us to teach, to share our knowledge and experiences with others.

Many business associates have contributed to this book, including colleagues at the Cherry Corporation where I held my first international position. In addition, I would like to thank the management and associates at Littelfuse Inc. who supported this work and graciously allowed me to use our company in my examples.

Finally, I would like to thank you, the reader. Your quest for knowledge and your desire to expand your business bridges cultures and brings the world closer together. The international businessperson is this world's new explorer and hopefully this book will be your guide.

George F. Seyk

Asia

Southeast Asia

East Asia

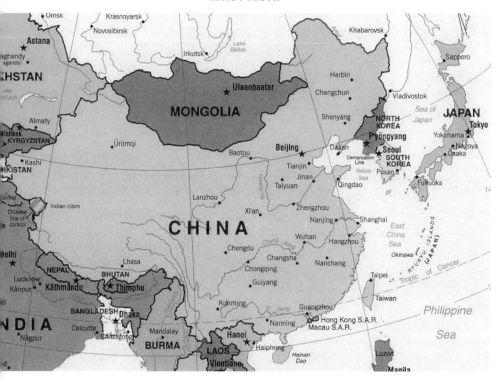

PART ONE

Marketing in Asia

1. Sizing up the Market
The Case of Bill Stafford

Bill Stafford, president and founder of MIB Corp., a successful U.S. company supplying cell phone components to American customers, saw his business grow as the telecommunications industry expanded. By maintaining solid customer relationships, providing innovative products and good local sales support, Bill believed the firm would have a promising future. That is, until one of his biggest clients dropped a bomb.

'It was just announced last week,' he told Bill, 'that because our market is getting very competitive, we will be setting up a factory in China near Suzhou to take advantage of lower production costs. We assume MIB will continue to support us and would like to know what your plans are for Asia.'

Bill's heart stopped. Asia?! China?! He hadn't expected this. Bill had trouble finding China on a map, let alone Suzhou. He wasn't sure what to do or say but pulled himself together and tried to appear calm.

'This is interesting news,' he replied. 'I would like more details regarding your timetable and decision. Obviously, we want to continue to support you wherever in the world you decide to locate facilities. Perhaps we should meet again to discuss how we can best support your new operations.'

The purchasing agent agreed and another meeting was scheduled. They shook hands and parted.

Bill had bought some time, but he was still off balance. On the plane trip home his mind raced. Asia! The place couldn't be further away from MIB company headquarters. The customer might as well move to the moon!

Questions started to fill Bill's mind. If this company was moving to Asia in order to become more competitive, then others in the industry would likely follow. He could visualize a major shift in business. Bill needed to respond or MIB's future would be in jeopardy.

But what to do? How should he plan; what variables should he consider? What product or price issues would he encounter? What about cultural issues? How do the Chinese behave and how do you negotiate with them? And sales networks. What channeling alternatives are available? Would there be legal issues to consider? How should all this be managed and what kind of people should manage it?

'On the other hand, perhaps this is an opportunity,' he thought. If he is the first supplier with his type of product in China, maybe he can 'out-position the competition.' Perhaps MIB could find new markets. Whatever the possibilities, Bill knew he had to be very careful and make his choices wisely.

MIB had suddenly become the victim of a major trend. In many industries companies are expanding globally, looking for sourcing and marketing opportunities in Asia. Expansion forces the suppliers of such companies to expand with them as well, in many cases building or shifting operations to remain close to customers or to take advantage of local resources. This development has profound implications for markets and supply channels.

Globalization and Asia

Though new to Bill, this trend is familiar to many business people. Your authors, who together have over thirty-five years of hands-on experience doing business in the Pacific Rim, address in this book the problems executives, associates, clients, and colleagues have experienced when buying, selling, or setting up a new business in Asia.

Trade with Asia is not new, of course. In the quest to expand business and make a deal, businessmen from outside the region have historically targeted Asia as a market. The motivation has always been to obtain new markets and/or resources. From a marketing standpoint, the goal is to take advantage of opportunities that will allow for growth and profit. Likewise, from a resource standpoint the goal is to leverage economies of scale that will enhance competitiveness. These two goals have always been the focus of any company seeking expansion in Asia.

Although trade with Asia is not new, new technology has definitely influenced how it is done. Take transportation for example. The world is not getting smaller – just ask any beleaguered traveler suffering from jet lag! But today most parts of Asia can be reached in less than twenty-four hours from almost anywhere in the world, making visiting Asian customers and delivering products to Asian markets easier and more efficient. High-speed transportation and networking have helped define what we now call the global supply chain.

New technology has also impacted communication. Phones, faxes, and computers help transcend time zones and expand opportunities. Today calling clients in Japan or Singapore is almost as easy as calling your neighbor. Although you cannot eliminate distance, technological development has given us powerful new tools to manage it.

Technology has also created new markets in Asia. China, for example, is now one of the largest users of cellular phones. Because the country lacked a traditional telecommunications infrastructure, it decided to by-pass older technologies and leap ahead to newer ones. The end result was the development of new industries and services, which in turn developed into brand new markets.

All of these technological developments have contributed to globalization; that is, the utilization and integration of worldwide resources, capabilities, and markets to benefit one's business. In this book we will use the terms international, multinational, and global interchangeably. How a company plans, utilizes available resources, and responds to multinational market needs will ultimately determine its success in a globalized economy.

Of all the regions in the world, few are more impacted by globalization than Asia. With its huge population and numerous resources, Asia is seen as a market opportunity by many industries. And well it should. Its population, per capita income, and savings are growing, resulting in more purchasing power and a rapidly expanding consumer market. The region offers expanded sales for existing products and potential sales for new products. Selling in Asia can also overcome saturated domestic markets. Some companies extend the lifecycle of mature products by entering the region. Others tap emerging new markets such as electronic commerce.

Now let's look at the geography of the Asia-Pacific region.

Asia: The Geography

Here are the geographic terms we use in this book:

East Asia:	Japan, Korea, China, Taiwan.
Southeast Asia:	Singapore, Malaysia, Thailand, Philippines, Indonesia, Brunei, Vietnam, Cambodia, Laos, Myanmar (Burma).

ASEAN: Association of Southeast Asian Nations (see
                          above).

South Asia: India, Pakistan, Sri Lanka, Nepal, and Ban-
                          gladesh.

'**Greater China**:'   The Peoples Republic of China (including
                          Hong Kong and Macao) plus Taiwan.

Pacific Rim: East and Southeast Asia, Australia/New
                          Zealand plus the Pacific coasts of Canada,
                          the United States, Latin America, and Rus-
                          sia.

Asia-Pacific Region: Pacific Rim plus South Asia.

Asia is a mosaic of different markets and differing business cultures.
Companies organize their Asian operations in various ways. For example, an American manufacturer of chemical and cleaning products
does it this way: East Asia, Japan and Korea; Greater China, encom-
passing the People's Republic of China (PRC), Taiwan and Hong
Kong; Central Asia, which includes India; and South East Asia, con-
sisting of Singapore, Indonesia, Malaysia, Philippines, Thailand,
Vietnam, Australia, and New Zealand. Other companies classify Japan
and Korea as North Asia or define the Peoples Republic of China as
a region unto itself because of its size.

Once we understand the geography we can take the next step:
making a plan.

Strategic Planning

Marketing success in Asia requires a lot of time and dedicated resources. Approaching the market necessitates ongoing learning and
research. Communication can be difficult, new sales channels are
often needed for successful market penetration. In addition, economic, political, cultural, and market variables can upset even the
soundest program. In sum, selling into the Asia-Pacific region can be
one of the greatest challenges a company will ever face.

Therefore, business people considering venturing into Asia must
ask themselves two questions. First, how fast and to what extent will

my business grow if we're not in Asia? Second, can we be competitive in our own market without entering the Pacific Rim?

The answers to these questions will help establish a business plan. No explorer goes into uncharted lands without contemplating why he or she is going there. Why should business be any different?

Strategic planning involves organizing ideas and goals in a concise list format.

One simple planning model may look as follows:

Steps For Strategic Planning

1. Assess the current situation
2. Set objectives
3. Determine trends
4. Establish opportunities
5. Recognize threats
6. Define strategy
7. Formulate a time line
8. Measure results

A more detailed planning model for determining the viability of entering the Asian market looks like this:

1. Identify customers who need your products or services
2. Find a competitive advantage for those products or services
3. Look for opportunities to profitably leverage your resources or know-how
4. Identify technological or service trends that you can exploit for success

The above should be weighed against potential barriers to market entry, which include:

1. Sales-channel availability and access
2. Cultural variables such as different languages, needs, and lifestyles
3. Legal restrictions and trade practices
4. Promotional limitations such as types of media or availability
5. Socioeconomic and cultural variables: population, education, income, norms, beliefs, and values

A critical part of the planning process entails defining a strategy, which involves the following elements:

The Mission: An overall guide for all aspects of your strategy, this is a product of analyzing your intentions for market participation.

Positioning: Integrating choices and competencies to attain maximum benefit and competitive advantage. Choices include market and geographic selection, business involvement, channel-entry method and/or service offering. Positioning also involves instructions on how to compete and to establish market recognition.

Resources: Determining what is needed to implement the strategy and ensure success of the positioning scheme by choosing which assets and competencies should be fused to accomplish your goals. Since your company's resources are usually limited, you will have to prioritize. In addition, you may need to acquire new competencies such as an understanding of Asian business cultures and negotiation techniques.

Structuring: How you structure your organization ultimately determines how well your resources will be applied to achieving your positioning strategy. Your structure can range from a simple export system to an integrated matrix of distributors, licensees, joint ventures, and subsidiaries. It requires setting up the internal processes, support systems, communication methods, and management system to be successful in the market. Structuring is an important key to success.

The above elements will vary depending on the particular Asian markets you decide to focus on. Remember, Asia consists of many different nations with different governmental and political structures, languages and cultures – all of which will influence business dramatically. Asian infrastructure varies from the sophisticated to the rudimentary. Economies range from highly developed economically, e.g. Japan, to developing, e.g. Indonesia. Political, financial, and monetary stability may vary widely between nations. Business methods and practices differ greatly. Behavioral expectations and modes of thought are diverse and often unclear to non-Asian business people.

Lack of proper planning causes serious problems – even for the largest and most sophisticated companies. Take Merrill Lynch for example. A world leader in financial services, Merrill decided to aggressively enter the Japanese retail brokerage market. They spent large amounts of money on advertising and took over some branches of a failed Japanese securities company to help facilitate market entry. But Merrill's retail operations have lost money since they started in Japan. Although the firm fell victim to some non-controllables, such as deregulated commission fees and strong competition from on-line brokers, Merrill's main troubles stemmed from the early stages of planning.

Merrill Lynch originally planned to present itself as a local company, but soon found itself struggling in its attempt to develop recognition with the Japanese public. Ads depicting the company's trademark bull confused people unfamiliar with the symbol. Some people thought that the bull was a cow and could not comprehend how a cow relates to financial services. Subsequent ads also failed. As of this writing Merrill Lynch's future in Japan is very uncertain.

Marketing in Asia: Dealing With the Uncontrollable

Planning aims to exert control over what we are doing. But marketing is filled with assumptions and guesswork that are affected by many variables, some of which cannot be controlled. This holds particularly true for Asia. 'Uncontrollable' factors must be carefully considered when setting up a strategy, with the understanding that you will have little influence over them.

In Asia, uncontrollables vary from country to country:

- Political forces, trade policies, and regulations governing foreign participation in local markets.
- Laws and regulations governing business setup and structure as well as competition, pricing, and human resource issues.
- Financial regulations controlling currency valuation and exchange risks.
- Tax laws.
- Infrastructure development, e.g. communication and transportation facilities.
- Geographic and climatic factors, including effects on labor productivity and logistics.
- Economic variables, e.g. market size, stratification, and buying power.

- Levels of technology, including what is acceptable in a given market.
- Structure of sales channels (in some cases channel availability itself).
- Competitive elements such as level, type, and number of local competitors.
- Cultural and sociological variables, including beliefs, habits, life styles, language, history, education, and social institutions.

You will need to consider all of these factors when marketing in Asia. Forces in a company's home country can also influence a marketing program in Asia, and may be equally uncontrollable. They may include domestic policies regarding trade with foreign countries, competition from local companies competing in Asia, financial issues, taxation, and legal concerns such as export and anti-trust laws. Equally important are cultural forces in one's own country since your home country's lifestyles, language, beliefs, expectations, and history can also inhibit international marketing campaigns. For instance, many Europeans are multi-lingual, giving European companies an advantage in international business compared to U.S. companies.

An extreme example of a local uncontrollable was the terrorist attack on the U.S. East Coast on September 11, 2001. As a result of those attacks, the United States government grounded air transportation and reopened it slowly over time. Many exporters to Asia thus faced an uncontrollable interruption in their shipment patterns and logistics networks. Businesses had to adjust and factor this uncontrollable into their further planning.

Although dealing with uncontrollables is challenging, it is not impossible. There are also many things we can control. We can control our strategy and how we plan. We can make appropriate changes in response to new information and forces. We can determine how to leverage corporate resources and invest in the market. We can control what products we manufacture and how to modify them to address local markets. We can also control how we promote and advertise our products or services and how we distribute our products, including methods of market access.

But most importantly, we can control ourselves. We can control how and what we learn. We can adapt to and bridge business cultures. Ultimately, our marketing success in Asia is determined by how well we manage what we can control. This is every company's challenge.

The Greatest Marketing Variable: People

Earlier we mentioned that technology is a driving force towards globalization. But technology does not solve all of the problems confronting business people marketing globally. As anthropologist Edward T. Hall noted, 'Technical solutions that can be applied to environmental problems can't be applied rationally until mankind transcends the intellectual limitations imposed by our institutions, our philosophies, and our cultures.' ['Beyond Culture' Anchor Books/Doubleday, 1976]. He wrote this before the term 'globalization' became popular. However, it is a challenge for every businessperson to transcend the limitations imposed by our philosophies, institutions, and cultures in order to successfully do business in other countries. This means successful international business people must understand cultural differences.

U.S. automobile manufacturers learned this when they started to export cars to Asia. Many companies offered Asian customers standard models that sold well in the USA. But many American cars were too big for narrow Asian streets and parking facilities, consumed too much fuel, which is much more expensive in Asia, and had steering wheels on the wrong side. The sales results were dismal because the cars had not been adapted to Asian conditions.

In contrast, international marketers who do understand local cultures succeed. For example, McDonald's changed eating habits throughout Asia with its food offerings and service style. It made hamburger and fries popular in places that had never before heard of such things. However, McDonald's also adapted their food offerings: no pork in Muslim countries, no beef or pork products in Hindu countries.

Understanding similarities as well as differences in culture and human behavior is important for marketing and negotiating in Asia. Proctor and Gamble influenced Chinese habits by introducing shampoo to that country. Previously, most Chinese hadn't used shampoo to wash their hair. They used soap. Now shampoo has gained popularity to the point of creating a new industry complete with local competitors. Proctor and Gamble helped change personal usage patterns, but they didn't significantly alter Chinese culture itself.

Asia consists of geographically, economically, politically, historically, sociologically, and psychologically diverse peoples. Differences can be overt or subtle. Japanese, Koreans, Chinese, Thai, Malays,

Filipinos are all Asians, but each group is culturally and socially unique with different beliefs, values, language, and business behavior. Even within these countries there are different subcultures and behavioral patterns.

To succeed in Asia the international marketer must know how to operate in this unique, complex multicultural environment.

2. Business Behavior in Asia
Three Keys to Understanding Asian Business Behavior

In this chapter we aim to provide a framework to help both Western-ers and Asians bridge the East-West culture gap that frustrates entre-preneurs and managers on both sides of the divide. Looking through Western eyes, we highlight three keys to understanding the way Asians conduct business – especially across the bargaining table:

- The importance of Relationships.
- The importance of Hierarchies.
- The use of Time.

Let's start by looking at the major role played by relationships and interpersonal connections throughout the Asia-Pacific region.

Relationships

Whether we are marketing, selling, sourcing, or negotiating a joint venture, the fundamental differences between relationship-focused and deal-focused business behavior impact our business success throughout the global marketplace. This is especially true for Asia.

Most of the world's business cultures are in fact relationship-ori-ented. Most Asians, Africans, Latin Americans and people from the Mediterranean region prefer to get things done by working with peo-ple with whom they have solid connections.

Being relationship-focused, Asians prefer to deal only with family, friends, and persons or groups well known to them – people who can be trusted. They are uncomfortable talking business with strangers, especially strangers who also happen to be foreigners. Because of this key cultural value, Asian firms typically want to know their prospec-tive business partners well before thinking about doing business with them.

In contrast, Westerners – especially those in northern Europe,

North America, Australia, and New Zealand – tend to be less wary of talking business with people they don't know. They are more deal-oriented. The following chart is our 'Who's Who' of relationship-focused and deal-focused business cultures.

Deal-focused business behavior:
- Anglo cultures: UK, USA, Canada, Australia, and New Zealand
- Northern Europe

Moderately deal-focused:
- Latin Europe, Central and Eastern Europe
- Chile, southern Brazil, northern Mexico
- Hong Kong, Singapore
- South Africa

Relationship-focused business behavior:
- Arab World, the Mediterranean region, most of Africa
- Most of Latin America
- Most of Asia

Making Initial Contact

Because Asians don't normally like to deal with strangers, smart marketers make the first approach to potential buyers or partners indirectly. One good way is to meet Asian counterparts at international trade shows. That's where buyers look for new suppliers, exporters seek importers, and investors search for partners. Business behavior at international shows and exhibitions tends to be somewhat deal-focused because those who attend are usually there for the express purpose of making new contacts.

Another good way is to join an official trade mission. All over the world today governments and trade associations organize guided visits of business people in order to open new markets. The trade-mission organizer makes appointments with interested parties and provides formal introductions to them. Introductions break the ice and smooth the way to a business relationship.

You can also arrange to be introduced by a third party, an intermediary. The ideal introducer in Asia is a high-status person or organization known to both parties. So if you happen to be good friends with a respected retired statesman who just happens to be well acquainted with one of your prospects, that's wonderful. Otherwise, a number of organizations are able to act as respected intermediaries.

For example, your country's trade representatives in the target market are usually able to provide introductions. Embassy and consular officials tend to be accorded high status in Asian cultures, and of course it's part of their job to promote your country's exports. Chambers of commerce, banks, trade associations, freight forwarders, ocean and airfreight carriers, international law and accounting firms are also potential introducers.

And don't forget that poker buddy of yours who works for a company with offices in Tokyo, Shanghai, and Mumbai. Try letting him win a big pot – maybe his firm will arrange a key introduction for you!

Recognizing the importance of third-party introductions in their home market, the Japanese External Trade Organization (JETRO) is willing to provide that service to reputable foreign companies. In fact, proper introductions are so critical that specialized consulting firms exist whose main function is to introduce *gaijin* [foreigners] to Japanese companies. Of course, using consultants is likely to cost you more than other ways of obtaining an introduction.

What About Telemarketing?

To illustrate the importance of the indirect approach for Asian marketing, let's use telemarketing as an example. In the United States people are bombarded every day at home and office by total strangers trying to sell something. You've heard of B2B (business to business) marketing? Well, in America telemarketing could be called S2S (stranger-to-stranger) marketing.

The direct sales approach works in America because the U.S. is the home of the cold call. Naturally, having an introduction or referral helps, but the enormous success of telemarketing firms proves they are not essential.

In contrast, Japanese marketers use the telephone to contact *existing* customers and partners, not for cold calls to new prospects. The direct phone-sales approach just doesn't work in Asian relationship-oriented societies. So the wise international marketer will remember that the shortest route to success in Asia is the indirect route.

The following case, reported by a participant at one of our U.S. negotiating workshops, shows what happens when a clueless exporter overlooks this fundamental fact.

Case: 'Locating a Distributor in Japan.'

Jim Adams was the busy international sales manager at CommTec, a telecommunications equipment manufacturer based in Kansas City. The day before departing to visit his company's Hong Kong distributor, Jim decided this would be a good opportunity to start looking for a good distributor in Japan – a market showing real potential. He had to change planes at Narita Airport anyway, so the Japan stop would cost little extra time and money.

His quick scan of databases turned up information on Nagoya Telecoms Industries Co. Ltd., a major importer and distributor of the same type of equipment CommTec was exporting to Hong Kong, Singapore, and Thailand. The data also showed that NTIC was currently importing similar equipment from Australia and Germany.

Jim was able to change his return flight to include a short visit to Nagoya. When Jim arrived he tried phoning NTIC from his hotel for an appointment, but the receptionist did not speak English. Finally he asked the hotel desk clerk to phone and in that way was able to confirm a meeting the next morning at 9:00 am.

At NTIC Jim met with two people, a woman in her 20s who spoke English and a man in his early 30s who communicated through the young woman. The atmosphere of the meeting was friendly enough, but Jim had trouble steering the conversation around to the topic that had brought him there: NTIC's possible interest in importing and distributing CommTec equipment.

After half an hour of pleasant general conversation the woman asked, 'How long are you staying in Nagoya?' and Jim replied he had to leave early the next day. After this, the two Japanese continued to smile but sat quietly and asked no more questions.

To get things moving again the American handed over two sets of his company's sales literature and suggested it was time to discuss business. The two NTIC employees conversed together for a minute or so in Japanese and then the woman told Jim they would review his brochures and get back to him if they had any interest.

Back in Kansas City Jim Adams sent follow-up emails but never did hear from NTIC. He was puzzled because CommTec products obviously fit into NTIC's range and were also priced competitively relative to Australian and German suppliers. 'Why no response?' he asked himself.

We explained to this new-to-market export salesman that in Asia, people get things done through relatives, friends, contacts, and connections. That is, through relationships. It really is 'who you know' that counts. The Chinese call these networks of personal connections *guanxi*, a word well-known throughout East and Southeast Asia.

Sure, knowing the right people helps anywhere in the world, but in the strongly relationship-oriented Asia-Pacific markets, the proven way to get started is to be referred or introduced by the right people or organization. Cold calls just do not work there.

Getting down to Business

How things proceed at the first meeting is also influenced by culture. While transaction-oriented people get down to business quickly, relationship-focused people like to take their time getting to know each other first. Asians say, 'First you make a friend. Then you make a deal.'

Why is this difference in meeting behavior so important for U.S. companies, for example? A recruitment ad which keeps appearing every few months in the Wall Street Journal provides a clue. It is an ad seeking 'one-call closers,' people who are able to sell a big-ticket intangible to prospects at the first meeting. Such an ad can only work in America, the world's most deal-focused culture.

Selling in Asia requires exactly the opposite approach. Once you're introduced you can expect a series of meetings devoted to relationship-building. Sure, you'll also talk business during these meetings – though in Japan often not at the initial get-together. But you certainly should not expect to 'close,' to 'ask for the sale' the first time you meet!

The vice-president of marketing for one of America's largest breweries was not briefed about this cultural trait before he flew to Tokyo. At his first meeting with Japan's largest importer-distributor of beverages, our friend expected to start talking business within five minutes or so, as he would in Milwaukee. After 20 minutes of small talk he began to fidget and look at his watch. After half an hour the U.S. executive cleared his throat and interrupted his counterparts to say, 'Gentlemen, if you don't mind, can we get down to business now? I have a busy day ahead of me ...'

There was an awkward silence, and then the boss of the Japanese company stood up. 'Ah, Smith-san, you've had a very tiring trip from the U.S. We'll take you back to your hotel for a rest.'

'Well thanks,' replied the marketing VP. 'But when do we get together to discuss the distribution agreement?'

'We'll call you,' came the smiling reply. But that call never came, and the American had to return empty handed. This U.S. brewery kept trying for over seven years without success to interest a Japanese distributor in importing their well-known brand. They finally cracked the market when they found a large retailer willing to import directly, thus bypassing the importers.

The brewery's management learned from the retailer why the importers were reluctant to do business with them. 'Lots of Japanese are uncomfortable talking business with people who do not take time to build rapport. Of course, we Japanese know this. It's only *gaijin* who have that problem.'

It takes time, patience and (sometimes a cast-iron liver) to develop strong relationships in East Asian markets such as Japan, South Korea, and Taiwan. Getting drunk together seems to speed up the rapport-building process – but normally only for men. While there are increasing exceptions these days, women as a rule don't fit in at these male-bonding drinking rituals.

Of course, building trust and rapport with your customer is important everywhere in the world, not only in relationship-oriented markets. The big difference is that with most Asians you have to develop that climate of trust *before* you start talking business. It also means that face-to-face contact is important. Even electronic communications has not reduced this need. Asians are less comfortable discussing important matters in writing, over the phone or via videoconferencing. They expect to see their suppliers and partners in person more often than is necessary in most Western markets.

In Asia, building rapport should always be the first step. This often causes problems for deal-oriented business people who rely heavily on written agreements to prevent misunderstandings and solve problems. Americans in particular tend to take a legalistic, contract-based approach when disagreements and disputes arise. Many U.S. negotiators bring a lengthy draft contract and a lawyer to the bargaining table with them and proceed to discuss the proposed agreement clause by clause, consulting their legal adviser every time a question arises. In most of Asia, however, a better approach is to keep the lawyers more in the background until the later stages of the discussions, conferring with them during breaks.

Of course, good legal advice is as important in Asia as anywhere else. The difference lies in the role of lawyers; how they should contribute to the negotiating process.

Direct vs Indirect Language

Deal-oriented Western business people tend to value direct, frank, straightforward language, whereas their Asian counterparts more often favor an indirect, subtle, roundabout style. In our experience, this communication gap is one of the greatest causes of misunderstandings between Asian and Western business people, because the two sides expect different things from the communication process.

When communicating with others, the top priority for task-focused business people is to be clearly understood. Most of the time they say what they mean and mean what they say. German and Dutch negotiators, for example, are well known for their very frank, blunt language.

On the other hand, Asian negotiators usually assign the highest priority to maintaining harmony and promoting smooth interpersonal relations. Because preserving harmony within the group is so important, Asians carefully watch what they say to avoid embarrassing or offending others.

East and Southeast Asian negotiators seem to treat 'no' as a four-letter word. To avoid insulting you they may murmur, 'That will be difficult' or 'We will have to give that further study.' Popular variations are 'Maybe' and 'That may be inconvenient.' They often smile and change the subject or simply say nothing at all. Silence during a meeting with East Asian negotiators often means no.

Richard Butler, the former chief UN arms inspector, was quoted in the New York Times of March 28, 1999 about his experiences as his country's ambassador to Thailand. 'I learned that when you want to make your main point, a point about which you may even be very angry, the Thai way is actually to go as quiet as possible. Really lower your voice. It's the opposite of what we in the West are taught ... And it works.'

Over the years we have noticed a similar paraverbal communication tactic in Japan. When the senior Japanese negotiator wishes to emphasize a very important point, he may lower his voice almost to a whisper. That can confuse European and American as well as Arab negotiators, who are more likely to raise their voice in the same situation.

'Inscrutable Oriental'?

Many Western negotiators find Asian indirectness and paraverbal behavior confusing. They say East and Southeast Asians are 'hard to read,' that they tend to hide their emotions – especially negative emotions. In Asia showing impatience, irritation, frustration, or anger disrupts harmony. It is rude and offensive. So people often mask negative emotion by remaining expressionless or by smiling.

Thais, for example, seem to smile all the time. They smile when they are happy, they smile when they are amused, they smile when they are nervous. They may even smile when they are absolutely furious. Thai people smile that way because to openly display anger would cause everyone concerned to lose face. So what some Weserners perceive as 'inscrutability' really reflects the Asian concern with maintaining harmony and not offending people.

'Face'

While Westerners associate the concept of 'face' primarily with East Asian and Southeast Asian societies, it is in fact a cultural universal. It's what Anglo-Saxons, for example, call self-respect. True, Asians do seem especially sensitive to face issues, perhaps because relationship-focused cultures are so group-oriented. More than with most Westerners, Asian self-image and self-respect depend very much on how they are viewed by other people.

That's why business visitors to the Pacific Rim need to be especially conscious of how their verbal and nonverbal messages may be interpreted. This case drawn from our negotiating experience in Asia may serve as a useful reminder.

Case: 'Negotiating in Shanghai.'

A 32 year-old sales engineer we'll call Bob Andretti was in Shanghai on his first visit to the PRC. He was there to negotiate a joint-venture (JV) agreement with a public-sector company. On the fourth day of meetings the two sides were discussing the factory equipment worth about US$7.5 million that Bob's company was to supply the JV.

At one point the American could see that the Chinese side apparently did not understand the shipping term 'Free on Board' (F.O.B.), thereby understating the value of the U.S. firm's contribution to the project.

To clear up the misinterpretation Bob turned to the Chinese company's 55 year-old senior engineer. 'Mr. Li, I guess you don't understand what we mean by F.O.B. Let me explain it to you briefly ...' Having smoothly corrected his counterpart's mistake, Bob expected the meeting to get back on track. But to his surprise, the Chinese negotiators suddenly seemed to lose interest in the proceedings and adjourned the meeting without setting a date for the next session.

Bewildered, Bob called his home office that evening to report that after a very promising beginning, negotiations were suddenly at an impasse. Participants in our negotiating seminars are asked two questions:

A. 'If you were to explain to Bob Andretti what happened to damage the atmosphere of the meeting, which explanation would you choose?
  1. The Chinese were unhappy because under Bob's interpretation of the delivery terms they would have to pay several hundred dollars more than originally anticipated.
  2. Bob was being much too formal. After three or four days of meetings it was high time for him to address the Chinese senior engineer by his first name.
  3. In correcting the leader of the Chinese team in an open meeting Bob had caused him to lose face.
  4. Bob's interpretation of 'F.O.B.' was in fact incorrect, and while too polite to argue, the Chinese were justifiably upset with Bob.

There is no information given in the case to support number 1 or 4. Seminar attendees usually agree that the best explanation is number 3: the young U.S. negotiator had unintentionally insulted his senior counterpart by correcting him in front of others.

B. 'How can visiting negotiators avoid this kind of negative outcome?'

To avoid causing loss of face, Bob should have called for a break, taken Mr. Li aside and quietly said something like, 'I am sorry that clause is so poorly written. What we meant is ...' By speaking one-on-

one and taking the blame on himself, Bob could have cleared up the misunderstanding without causing his high-status Asian counterpart to lose face.

Another real-world case of a cross-cultural misunderstanding involving face comes from a participant in one of our recent University of Wisconsin Executive Education workshops.

Case: 'Managing Asian Distributors: Thailand'

As your firm's new export manager, you face a big problem in your largest Pacific Rim market: Thailand. Your Thai distributor is doing a very good job of moving 'Thunder Bucket' whirlpool baths in a tough market. Even now, despite the recent sharp devaluation of the baht, Chiang Mai Imports remains your best-performing Asian distributor.

The problem is a complete breakdown in communication. It all started a week before you took over exports, during a routine phone conversation. Frank Blunt, technical support specialist for the Thunder Bucket bath line, called the boss of Chiang Mai Imports, Aya Pornchai – daughter of CMI's late founder.

Khun Aya had faxed an urgent question that day concerning installation, and Frank phoned her back right around noon. That was quick response, but Aya seemed a little slow on the uptake – maybe because it was midnight in Bangkok. In view of the urgency Frank got right to the point, telling Aya that her question was answered quite clearly on page 31 of the Installation Manual.

After a pause, the managing director of CMI replied slowly, 'Well, I'm afraid that particular paragraph is not clear to us over here. That's why I faxed you for a clarification.'

By that time it had already been a very long day. Frank was half an hour late for his lunch date with the new secretary in Logistics. Exasperated, Blunt replied: 'Hey, I rewrote that whole section last month myself. Wanted to make sure customers know how to connect the binary pump with the analog escutcheon. Why don't you try reading the manual once!'

This time there was a longer pause followed by some one-syllable words Frank took to be Thai, and then came a busy signal. Assuming it was just another problem with the Bangkok phone system, Frank redialed the number, but nobody picked up.

Since that phone call, Khun Aya has absolutely refused to talk with Frank Blunt – the guy with all the answers. Instead she pesters you with questions that you have to refer to Frank. You've had enough experience over the years doing business with Asians to know that if your relationship with CMI's boss were stronger, you'd be able to smooth things over somehow.

But unfortunately, you're new to the job; you've only spoken with Khun Aya over the phone. What do you do now?

In small-group discussions, seminar participants with business experience in Asia usually conclude correctly that the new export manager should get on a plane at the first opportunity to meet with Khun Aya. A few days of face-to-face relationship building plus a good Thai translation of the manual will smooth things over. Oh yes, and how about some intercultural communication training for Frank Blunt?

As these cases demonstrate, variations in verbal and nonverbal behavior do indeed cause culture clashes. But a skilled interpreter can smooth over potential problems. That's what is going on when an interpreter takes several minutes to render in Japanese or Chinese what a Western visitor just said in a couple of short sentences. In Asia, part of the translator's task is to cloak overly-direct statements with the proper amount of polite, diplomatic circumlocution.

The Meaning of 'Sincerity'

As a final example of the differences in communication styles, let's look at contrasting meanings of the word 'sincerity.' To English speakers from deal-focused parts of the world, sincerity connotes honesty and frankness. A sincere friend for instance is one who tells you the truth even when that truth happens to be unpleasant.

In contrast, for Asian negotiators a 'sincere' friend is someone who is willing to be helpful. For example, to agree to a better price, to accept a late delivery, to make a generous compromise on a claim. A Western negotiator who truthfully reports her inability to shave another five percent off the price may well be thought of as 'insincere'.

Asian Hierarchies: Status, Power, and Respect

Anthropologists tell us that all human societies exhibit hierarchical tendencies. Scandinavians and Australians are among the least hierarchical cultures, while Asian cultures count among the most hierarchical.

Asia-Pacific societies tend to be organized in steeply vertical hierarchies reflecting sharp differences in status and power. This trait can cause problems for Western negotiators who don't know how to show respect to high-status local counterparts – especially customers. In most parts of Asia, status increases markedly with one's age as well as one's rank in the company. And in many Asian cultures buyers have higher status than sellers.

Potential Asian customers may be offended by the breezy familiarity of visitors from informal, relatively egalitarian Western societies.

Informal cultures:
- Australia
- Scandinavia
- USA
- Canada, New Zealand

Formal cultures:
- Most of Europe and Asia
- Mediterranean region, the Arab world
- Latin America

Since social hierarchies exist everywhere, just how important are status differences in Asia? The most obvious case is perhaps the caste system of India, but our favorite example is one we witnessed on a six-hour flight from Tokyo to Singapore. Seated in business class, we wondered about the several Japanese business men who repeatedly walked from economy to first class and back again.

The experienced Singapore Airlines flight attendant solved the mystery. 'They're all from the same big Japanese company. The president is sitting up front, two vice presidents are here in Business, the four other guys are back in Economy. I guess they need to discuss what they are going to do tomorrow in Singapore.'

That experience helps us remember the importance of showing

respect to the most senior person at a business meeting in Asia. We greet that person first, seat him (usually a male) in the place of honor, and focus much of our attention on him during the meeting.

Playing the Name Game: The First May Be Last

Addressing people formally is another important way of showing respect in hierarchical cultures. Some Australians and Americans need reminding that Asian counterparts should be addressed by family name, plus title or honorific as appropriate, rather than by their given name.

Note: In East and Southeast people refer to 'given' name instead of 'first' name, and 'family' name or surname instead of 'last' name. That's because with Chinese, Koreans and Japanese the family name precedes the personal name or names. This tradition helps us remember the great importance of the family in Asian cultures.

The following are some general rules of the name game. For detailed guidance check out the culture-specific profiles in Part II as well as the references in the Further Readings list.

Country	Name	Refer to as:
Greater China	Yi Er San	Mr. Yi, Chairman Yi.
Japan	Tanaka Koji	Mr. Tanaka, Tanaka-san.
Korea	Park Yeon Sung	Mr. Park, General Manager Park.
Philippines	Martin Coronel	Mr. Coronel
Indonesia (Java)*	Widodo	Mr. Widodo
Malaysia	Ismail bin Yacob	Encik (Mr.) Ismail
Thailand	Somchai Gobpradit	Khun (Mr.) Gobpradit
India		
- Hindu, north:	Narinder Lall	Mr. Lall
- Hindu, south:	Siva Murugan	Mr. Siva
- Muslim:	Ali bin Osman	Mr. Ali
- Sikh:	Kuldip Singh	Mr. Singh, Mr. Kuldip Singh

(*Javanese often have only one name.)

Showing Respect to the Customer

All over the world today the customer is king. That's particularly true in Asia – except for Japan, where the customer is GOD! American sales people joke about playing 'customer golf,' meaning we're supposed to let the buyer win the game. Well, in Asia sales people often have to do much more than that.

The expat manager of a Western pharmaceutical company marketing to physicians in Japan found this out when he learned how his local sales force operated. His salesmen had to wash their prospects' cars, walk their dogs and do their grocery shopping before they could get an appointment to see the doctor.

In many Asian markets it's especially important to show deference to government officials, who enjoy high status throughout the region. The following case shows why this is important in South Asia.

Case: 'Negotiating with a Government Minister in Bangladesh'

A consultant with 20 years of experience in South Asia arranged for his U.S. client to meet the Minister for Textiles in connection with the client's plans to import garments from Bangladesh. The American company was asking the government for a favorable decision on a complex regulatory issue involving import quotas. The minister had considerable discretionary authority concerning this issue.

(The client was not optimistic. A major competitor who had made a similar and equally legitimate request a month earlier had been kept waiting for a week in Dhaka and had then been turned down by mid-level bureaucrats. That client was left wondering how he would handle the inevitable request for a substantial bribe.)

It was 45 degrees Celsius (113 degrees Fahrenheit) and very humid in Dhaka, but for some reason the minister's shiny new room air conditioner was not operating. This caused the visitors discomfort: at the consultant's insistence they were dressed in dark wool suits with starched shirts and somber ties.

The two Americans sat dripping sweat while the minister chattered away, cool and comfortable in lightweight white muslin. After an hour and a quarter of what seemed to be aimless chatter, the minister stood up and with a smile informed the visitors that he had decided to rule in their favor.

Back in the hotel getting ready to celebrate, the consultant got a phone call from the minister's personal assistant. 'Congratulations! By the way, thought you'd like to know that His Excellency's air conditioner is running perfectly well as we speak. He just decided not to turn it on during your visit. You will know why, I suppose?'

In our international negotiating seminars we present participants with these discussion-group questions:

1. Why did the consultant insist on dressing so formally?
2. Why did the minister keep the Western visitors sweating in a sweltering office when he could have turned on the window air conditioner?
3. Why do you think the client got the decision he wanted without paying 'baksheesh'? (A bribe. Also means a tip as well as alms for a beggar.)

The long history of European colonial domination in South Asia explains part of the story, the high status of government officials there the rest. This meeting gave the minister a chance to test the Western supplicants' willingness to show appropriate deference.

Wearing a suit and tie to meetings during the hot season sends a positive signal of respect; keeping one's jacket on in a non-airconditioned office signals even greater respect. The visiting negotiators passed the test – and lost two kilos (over four pounds) each as well!

Some Australian, Scandinavian, and North American managers attending our seminars point out that they are at a disadvantage globally because of this cultural trait. Their competitors from hierarchical cultures already know all about formality, status differences and how to show respect, while those from egalitarian societies may not.

These managers have a valid point. A key rule of international business protocol is that when in an unfamiliar situation, err on the side of formality. That means for instance addressing people by their surname and title rather than given name, dressing more formally, and following local etiquette when shaking hands and exchanging business cards. In Part II we provide detailed information on business protocol for the major Asian markets.

Gender and Age Barriers

As in other hierarchical societies, Asians tend to ascribe status according to one's age, gender, and organizational rank. Therefore a young female negotiator may have difficulty being treated seriously in the region. Our next case, from a very large European multinational, deals with just such a situation.

Case: 'Negotiating in South Korea'

Since few women have reached positions of authority in local companies, many Korean men are unaccustomed to dealing with females on the basis of equality in a business context. Women therefore may face a significant cultural obstacle when trying to do business with Koreans. This is true even for buyers, despite the fact that Koreans generally treat customers with great respect.

Waldtraut Braun, 30-year old senior procurement manager from one of Germany's largest and best-know companies, was on her first visit to Seoul. Accompanied by Paul Schmidt, one of her male subordinates, she was there to negotiate a major purchase of industrial components. Since this South Korean manufacturer had been a supplier to her company for several years, Frau Braun expected the discussions to proceed without particular difficulty.

However, it did not work out that way. Throughout the meeting the Korean negotiators ignored her completely, addressing all questions and comments to Paul Schmidt. Furthermore, when Schmidt excused himself for a comfort break the Korean negotiators fell silent and acted as though Frau Braun was not there at all.

Frustrated by the way she was being treated, Frau Braun terminated the meeting before agreement could be reached and returned to her Singapore regional head office determined never again to negotiate with Koreans. Shortly thereafter this very successful purchasing manager arranged for a transfer to another division of her global company.

1. What cultural factor(s) may explain the way Frau Braun was treated in Seoul?
2. Should her company have sent a male buyer to Korea instead?

3. What practical steps could her company have taken to change the way Frau Braun was treated?
4. What could she herself have done before and during the Seoul meetings?

American managers must of course answer question number 2 in the negative: it is illegal for U.S. employers to make assignment decisions on the basis of gender.

Had her German company introduced her properly, and perhaps sent a senior male manager to join her at the first meeting, Frau Braun would have had a much easier time. As for her own behavior at this meeting, she should have instructed Herr Schmidt not to respond when spoken to, but instead to silently turn and look at her. In our experience, the Korean negotiators would have clearly understood this nonverbal message and acted accordingly. Failure to do any of these things led to a most unfortunate situation.

Another recent case provided by a Chicago workshop participant shows that the gender issue can even impact American companies doing business domestically with U.S. subsidiaries of some East Asian firms.

Case: 'Culture Clash in California'

During the early 1990s the California-based subsidiary of a large Japanese multinational phoned Big Six Inc., their accounting firm. They wanted a team of CPAs to spend a week or two on site to review current accounting procedures and recommend changes.

Jake Smythe of Big Six responded quickly. After all this was their largest client. Within a few days Jake had assembled a team of five experienced CPAs and sent them over to the client's office.

Two hours later Jake got a call from Mr. Saito, the client company's chief financial officer. 'Mr. Smythe, thank you for your quick response to our request. However, this team is not quite right for our firm. Would you kindly ask them to return to your office? Then please fax us a list with the full names of the accountants you would like to send in their place.'

Taken completely by surprise, Jake asked the client what was the problem with the first group. 'Mr. Saito, these are some of our very best people. They are all highly qualified and experienced accountants. For example, Paula Wiley and Glenda Roberts have both been with us for over ten years. And Mary Bennett ...' Jake paused as he heard Mr. Saito cough gently.

'Oh, I am sure they are all well qualified. And I am so sorry to cause you any trouble. But you see Mr. Smythe, some of our senior people here would feel more comfortable with ... ah ... you know, with male accountants. Please understand, some of our managers are not accustomed to working with female professionals. May I ask how long it will take for you to send over a new team?'

Saito was obviously embarrassed, but just as obviously dead serious about the gender issue. Jake knows he cannot afford to lose his biggest client. On the other hand he does not believe in making assignments on the basis of gender. What should he do?

Jake Smythe can try a face-to-face meeting with Saito-san. If the Japanese expat manager still refuses to accept the female accountants, Smythe has to choose between violating U.S. law and risking loss of a major customer. Our advice was to carefully explain the law in question to Mr. Saito, and if necessary perhaps offer to include a token male with the CPA team.

As more and more Western companies employ women in international sales and marketing positions, the gender issue increases in importance. So let's look at a recent success story:

Case: 'Kathy's Excellent Adventure'

Kathy was a 28 year-old materials engineer with a mid-sized U.S. electronics manufacturer on her first visit to East Asia. She was there to help Fred, the 47 year-old international sales manager, conduct new-product introductions and training sessions for their firm's Pacific Rim customers. Fred had been visiting and working with these companies for several years.

Although excited by this new challenge, Kathy was also somewhat concerned that her youth and gender might reduce her effectiveness in the Pacific Rim. Top management shared this concern, but agreed to send the young woman when Fred assured them that she would be accepted. The plan was to visit Hong Kong first and then Taiwan, South Korea and Japan.

Coached by Fred, Kathy carefully studied the business cultures involved, had new business cards printed to reflect her academic credentials, and put together a professional presentation focused on their customers' technical needs. The seminars in Hong Kong, Taiwan and Korea went smoothly even though on two occasions Kathy had to present the training sessions on her own, since Fred was busy elsewhere.

The first Japan visits also went well, with the two Americans accompanied by personnel from their company's local agent. Kathy also made a presentation to the Japanese agency's salesmen. Finally it was time to visit the last of the Japanese customers. Since he had a scheduling conflict, Fred suggested to Mr. Yamamoto, head of the Japanese agency, that Kathy conduct this session without him.

'Oh, that would be most difficult,' responded Yamamoto. In the event, the visit to that customer did not take place. Instead Mr. Yamamoto asked Kathy to make a second presentation to his sales people that day. 'Some of them didn't quite get it the first time,' he explained to her with a smile. Nevertheless, on the plane back to the U.S. Kathy couldn't help wondering about that sudden change in plans.

At our workshops we ask participants a number of questions about this case, which comes from our personal experience of marketing in Asia:

1. Why was Fred confident that Kathy would be well accepted by their East Asian customers despite the low status often accorded young people, and particularly women, in some of those cultures?

Fred expected few problems because he had been working with these companies for several years: a key consideration in the relationship-oriented business cultures of Asia.

2. Why did Kathy modify her business cards?

In addition to being relationship-focused, all four of the cultures they were to visit are also hierarchical. Kathy's academic credentials enhanced her status, making her more acceptable as a business partner.

3. Why do you think Fred arranged the visits in that particular order?

Women in business tend to be more easily accepted in Greater China than in Korea and Japan. Freed foresaw that her early successes in

Hong Kong and Taiwan would build her confidence in preparation for the challenges likely to face her in North Asia.

4. What do you suppose was the reason one of the Japan visits was canceled?

Despite Fred's strong relationship with that customer, management told Mr. Yamamoto in no uncertain terms that they did not want to be lectured by a woman. That reaction was unexpected, but Fred knew there is a margin of error in predicting business behavior anywhere in the world. The savvy international marketer must always be ready to 'roll with the punches.'

5. Why did Mr. Yamamoto arrange a repeat presentation for his sales people?

Ever sensitive to issues of face, the Japanese agent sought to spare Kathy's feelings by immediately proposing an alternate activity when her visit to their customer was canceled. The management of the Japanese customer was also concerned to save Kathy's face, achieving this by communicating the cancellation through an intermediary – Mr. Yamamoto. All this politeness worked: Kathy found out the reason for the change in plans only later, from Fred.

Time Behavior in Asia

Culture also influences how business people look at time and scheduling. In rigid-time societies such as Germany, punctuality is vital, schedules are firmly adhered to and meetings are seldom interrupted. U.S. anthropologist Edward T. Hall coined the useful term 'monochronic' for this type of culture.

Then there are what Hall terms 'polychronic' cultures, where people place less emphasis on punctuality and strict adherence to deadlines, and where business meetings may be constantly interrupted by phone calls and drop-in visitors.

These contrasting attitudes toward time regularly cause friction and misunderstanding when monochronic and polychronic negotiators meet in South and South East Asia. The chart below illustrates the varying orientations to time around the world.

Monochronic Business Cultures (in descending order):
- Germany and German Switzerland
- Northern Europe, North America, Australia/New Zealand
- Japan

Moderately Monochronic:
- Singapore, Hong Kong, Taiwan, China
- South Korea
- Russia, Southern Europe, most of East-Central Europe

Polychronic Business Cultures:
- The Arab World, most of Africa
- Most of Latin America
- South and Southeast Asia

Orientation to time may vary significantly within a country as well. Business people in the more industrialized coastal provinces of China tend to be more clock-conscious than those in the interior. And your South Korean meeting is more likely to start on time if it takes place in Seoul than in a small town in the countryside.

Where the Clock Slows Down

In polychronic, fluid-time cultures business people may be tardy for your meeting because they had to help a friend or family member solve a problem, or because an earlier meeting ended later than expected. Polychronic people consider it rude to end an ongoing meeting just because they happen to have another one scheduled now.

Indonesians have a delightful expression for polychronic time. *Jam karet* translates as 'rubber time,' which means visitors should expect flexible, stretchable meeting times and schedules. Indonesians tend to place a higher value on human relationships than on arbitrary schedules and deadlines.

The following example of polychronic culture shock comes from a seminar in Kuala Lumpur in the early 1990s.

Case: 'Waiting in Frankfurt.'

As the Malaysian manager of a Kuala Lumpur company marketing travel services, you are in Europe for a busy week of sales meetings.

On Monday you have an appointment in Frankfurt, on Tuesday in Oslo, Wednesday in Copenhagen, Thursday in Amsterdam and so on.

Due to flight delays you arrive very late on Sunday, suffer from jet lag and oversleep on Monday morning. Then the German taxi driver misunderstands your directions and takes you to an address on Eckenheimer Landstrasse instead of Eschersheimer Landstrasse. The result is that you arrive an hour and 45 minutes late for your 9 a.m. appointment at Dr. Jürgen Schmidt's office.

At the reception desk you explain you are late but you still need to meet with Dr. Schmidt, even if it has to be for a shorter time. Just then an unsmiling Dr. Schmidt enters the reception area carrying a briefcase and greets you formally. 'Well, good morning! Are you all right?' he asks, looking at you closely.

You apologize for being late and explain the confusion with the street addresses. 'Yes, I can understand that,' Dr. Schmidt replies, glancing at his watch. 'Unfortunately, however, I have to leave right now for our quarterly board meeting, and that will take the rest of the day. But since you came from so far away I'll try to rearrange my Tuesday schedule.' He checks his Palm Pilot and then asks, 'Can you come back at 11:00 a.m. tomorrow?'

You thank him but explain that you have a meeting in Oslo at 11:30 a.m. tomorrow. 'But I will be back in Frankfurt late Friday to take my return flight on Saturday afternoon. Could we perhaps get together Saturday morning for an hour or so?'

Dr. Schmidt seems to be somewhat surprised at your suggestion. 'That won't be possible,' he answers. 'Sorry it did not work out this time.' Then he shakes hands briskly and hurries out the door, leaving you to wonder just what happened.

1. Dr. Schmidt felt insulted by your lack of punctuality and decided to brush you off.
2. He is a rude, insensitive person, unwilling to make allowances for a visitor who has traveled a very long distance to see him.
3. A typical monochronic German, he does not want to deal with people who are so unreliable they come to a meeting almost two hours late.
4. He really did have a board meeting scheduled, and tried to help by offering to squeeze you in to his schedule the next day.
5. Most Germans do not work on weekends and usually have family activities planned for Saturday and Sunday.

The Malaysian woman who indignantly related this incident at one of our Kuala Lumpur seminars assumed that options 1, 2 and 3 accurately described her German counterpart's behavior that morning in Frankfurt. However, based on the information she gave, numbers 4 and 5 fit the situation better.

Germans typically smile less during initial business encounters than Southeast Asians, so Dr. Schmidt wasn't necessarily angry. The German manager probably had scheduled her for an hour or so and then planned to attend the board meeting. He tried to accommodate the Malaysian visitor by fitting her into his Tuesday schedule, but in all likelihood preferred to keep the weekend free for family activities.

Obviously the visitor should have phoned to report the delay and extend an apology, but in the event probably would have missed meeting Dr. Schmidt anyway, due to her late arrival at his office.

Western visitors are equally prone to culture shock when doing business in South and South East Asia. We often hear northern Europeans and North Americans complain about the 'rude behavior' of some business contacts and especially bureaucrats in those regions. 'Officials always keep me waiting and then continually interrupt the meeting to take phone calls and receive unscheduled visitors.'

So for balance, let's look a case of monochronic culture shock, this one from a 1998 seminar conducted in Herning, Denmark.

Case: 'Waiting in Bangalore'

Jesper Knudsen, owner of a Danish manufacturer of silk garments, planned to invest in a modern raw-silk fabric-weaving and dyeing mill in India. He asked an Indian consultant with good connections in the textile branch to help by arranging an appointment with the Minister of the Silk Industry.

The meeting was arranged in Bangalore, center of Indian silk manufacturing. Knowing how eager the Indian government was for this kind of investment, the Dane was looking forward to a warm welcome and a discussion of various incentives.

The Danish investor arrived for the meeting punctually at 9:00 a.m. But the consultant's flight was delayed, so he arrived at 10:15 a.m., just in time for the two to be ushered into the office of Minister S. Nagarajan. The meeting was a lively one. The Silk Minister carried on a disjointed conversation with Jesper, interrupted as he was by frequent phone calls, office boys bringing papers to sign, and visitors dropping in to chat.

After an hour or so, the Silk Minister stood up and shook hands with the puzzled Danish visitor. 'You will have no problems here, Mr. Knudsen,' he said with a broad smile.

Out in the hall the red-faced industrialist pulled the consultant aside. 'Rajesh, what a waste of time this was! I'm cancelling the rest of my trip right now and flying back to Herning. I thought the Indian government really wanted foreign investment here! I refuse to deal with rude, inefficient people who keep you waiting for over an hour and then interrupt you every few seconds to pick up the phone, sign papers, or chat with other visitors.'

Regretting that his delayed arrival had prevented him from briefing the Dane on what to expect at the meeting, the consultant began to think. 'How could I have explained things so that my client would not have been so upset at this important meeting?'

It is interesting that this case came to us from the very Indian consultant-professor involved, though his name has been changed to protect the guilty. Being Indian, 'Rajesh' should of course have aniticipated flight delays and cancellations. That was his real mistake. In all probablility he would have thoroughly explained polychronic meeting behavior to his client had he arrived in time.

What a pity – the meeting was actually a success! The minister had in fact given his blessing to the project, enabling all sides to proceed as planned.

As monochronic business travelers, here are two things we can do to avoid frustration during meetings in polychronic cultures:

- Take a briefcase filled with the paperwork and reports we never seem to find time to read. Instead of just sitting in the reception area twiddling thumbs, compulsively looking at our watch and muttering curses, try to put the time to good use.
- Pack a lot patience as well. Business meetings in much of South and Southeast Asia march to the beat of a slower drummer.

3. Laying the Groundwork
Preparation and Research

Preparation and research are extremely important to negotiating and marketing in Asia. How well we prepare directly influences success. Many companies embark on doing business in Asia without giving enough thought to preparation. They end up leaving things to chance, or try to tackle problems as they arise, resulting in failure or unnecessarily high costs.

Preparation entails having a method for gathering market intelligence and deciding on entry mode and organizational alternatives. There are two stages to market research in Asia. First we determine what to evaluate, then learn how to obtain reliable information.

Here are key elements to evaluate when marketing in Asia:

- Competition and competitive practice
- Political situation
- Economic condition
- Country infrastructure
- Trade barriers
- Local legal systems
- Local business orientation and practices
- Cultural variables (customs, habits, language, beliefs, religion, and the like)
- Financial conditions
- Local buying patterns
- Market size
- Government restrictions
- Available sales channels and entry vehicles
- Promotional methods
- Marketing costs and considerations
- Product or service needs
- Pricing level and trends

Market research comes down to understanding your customers' needs as well as you know your own business. Anticipating what customers want obviously helps you decide on a positioning strategy in Asia. Equally important is anticipating the actions of competitors and their impact on business. However, the biggest single issue regarding market research in Asia is obtaining and managing market intelligence. Reliability, sources, and accessibility of information present major challenges

In Asia, there are both formal and informal methods of research. Research requirements and methods vary from one market to another. For example, Japan and Korea maintain accurate market and trade data, much of which is available through government and industry organizations. That is the good news. The bad news for most Western marketers is that most of the information is in Japanese and Korean, so accessing the data requires researchers with local language capabilities.

Formal sources of information include:

– Industry and government data (e.g. import/export statistics)
– Libraries
– Business and trade materials: catalogs, product specifications, patent and intellectual property records
– Competitors' press releases, position papers or speeches
– Newspaper or magazine articles
– Business reports and industry analyst assessments
– Academic publications
– Embassies
– Chambers of Commerce
– Banks, advertising agencies and financial institutions
– Consultants and independent research firms

Local or provincial Asian governments trying to attract foreign investment can provide data. This is true in China, for example, where regional authorities compete with each other for investment. Other sources of information include trade missions and trade shows. Today, the Web and electronic data sources are also widely used for gathering information. Some of the best data may be in the local language, so hiring local talent to help research may be necessary.

Informal methods of obtaining data can complement formal ones. In some Asian countries informal methods are the best way to get information, depending on the industry or market that is being targeted. Developing countries present particular problems in this regard. China, for example, lacks many of the formalized data systems found in other countries in the region. Lack of reliable market intelligence is a major reason why so many companies fail in China. They enter the market with exaggerated expectations based on population size, only to realize later that market acceptance, maturity, timing, and access are major impediments.

Gathering competitive intelligence often requires just traveling around, talking to people first hand, visiting the target regions and markets. First-hand research is a key way of obtaining competitive intelligence. One company in Japan measured a competitor's production by counting cars in the parking lot. Because the location of the factory was far away from public transportation, most workers had to drive to the plant. The make and model of the vehicle indicated whether the driver was likely to be an assembly worker or manager. Depending on the vehicle mix and how many showed up, the company was able to estimate production output at given times.

A Chinese firm used another variation to this approach. This company counted sea containers leaving from a competitor's factory, estimating production by how many were shipped out in a week. They also figured out shipping destinations with a little work researching export documentation and records.

While market research impacts every aspect of doing business in Asia, it is particularly important for making product and pricing decisions.

Product Decisions:
The Fundamentals for Market Development

Two core decisions marketers face in Asia have to do with product selection and pricing. What a company sells and how much it gets for it are the cornerstones of success. Mistakes made in these areas are costly, and in some cases cause companies to fail in Asia.

When making product decisions, here are the key issues to consider:
– Product acceptability in the particular Asian market
– Selling features and brand-name decisions
– Labeling requirements, packaging or repackaging needs
– Service needs, warranty factors
– Legal issues such as patents, trademarks, trade names, and copyrights

Another variable is the effect of culture on product decisions. Of particular concern is the need for market adaptation: making products more acceptable to local demands, tastes, or expectations. Failure to address this issue can lead to costly mistakes.

Asia includes a vast array of cultures and therefore a large variety of consumer tastes, which is why products often need adaptation to be successful in Asia. The best example is the food industry. Campbell's Soup, for instance, markets an entire range of corn soup made exclusively for Greater China. And while pizza is popular in Asia, the toppings differ greatly by country. Shrimp is very popular in Southeast Asia, as are seaweed pizza in Japan and kimchi pizza in Korea.

Some companies which have identified specific market needs develop and sell products made especially for Asian markets. However, most manufacturers entering Asia don't start out that way. Instead they take a standard domestic core product and first attempt to market it to Asia 'as is'. From a business standpoint there are good reasons to begin with this approach. First, to minimize costs – product development costs money. Economies of scale are realized if common materials, processes, or equipment can be used to manufacture the products. After-sales service benefits from using common replacement parts and procedures.

A brand image acceptable in Asian cultures is helpful for marketing a core product in the region. This is particularly true in apparel retail where designer clothing and sportswear convey status or perceived quality, a factor that has benefited Fila and Levi's jeans. Mercedes, Harley-Davidson, Rolex watches and cigarette brands such as Marlboro, Kent, and Salem have benefited in a like manner.

Many component manufacturers enter the Asian market when their customers move production from North America and Europe to various countries in Asia in order to reduce costs. In some cases, these components are standardized globally, in other cases, they are modified for Asian requirements.

Companies use various strategies to position a product in Asia. Some make few changes to the product itself, and position it using the same brand name. Manufacturers from food items to industrial equipment have taken this approach, which is effective when the brand-name is recognized worldwide: e.g. Coca Cola, Budweiser, M&M's, Hershey's, and Kodak.

A variation of this approach is where a company maintains a common corporate identity and sells standart products as well as localized products in the Asian market. Food retailers such as McDonald's, Haagen Dazs, and Starbucks are good examples. In fact, McDonald's has been so successful that now a substantial part of the corporation's revenue comes from Asia. Japan alone has more than 3,500 McDonald's restaurants.

Another approach involves offering the same or similar product but under different names or brands. This is usually done to differentiate the product in some fashion (e.g. quality or price) and adapt it to different market segmentations. Apparel and cosmetic companies often employ this type of strategy within Asia. For example, one Japanese company offers certain brands of cosmetics only in Japan while marketing similar products under different brand names for export elsewhere in the region. Similarly, Proctor and Gamble sells 'Rejoice' shampoo in China, while 'Pert' is the brand name in the U.S.

Many products need to be modified to succeed in Asia. The way they look, are packaged, labeled, branded, and displayed are obvious variables. Other aspects entail more research and experience. Computers are a good example. Most computers sold in Asia have a common platform similar to computers sold in other world markets but are usually modified and configured to specifically meet Asian user needs, such as having Asian-language keyboards or being capable of utilizing unique or multi-language software.

Modifying packaging is an important consideration. In fact, packaging gets many companies into trouble in Asia. One U.S. firm spent millions of dollars promoting laundry detergent in Japan. Sales were nowhere near expectation, however, because the 'large economy-size boxes' that were so popular in the U.S. were too big for tiny Japanese retail stores and homes.

In Japan, aesthetics is often just as important as how well a product works. Foreign car manufacturers discovered this fact when they started exporting automobiles to Japan. Consumers there consider small quality imperfections in paint or in parts alignment sufficient cause for rejection. Even the paint under the hood needs to be perfect. Add to this special features requested by Japanese buyers, such as fold-up side view mirrors for narrow streets, or features such as warning devices required by the Japanese government, and you now have a unique automobile. Because of aesthetics alone, many companies selling into Japan – from large equipment makers to small components manufacturers – utilize a local or secondary inspection process just to ensure that their products adhere to the appearance- and quality-expectations of Japanese consumers. In fact, in Japan a whole industry is devoted to product inspection.

Size and format standards also play key roles in product acceptance because they vary from one Asian country to the next. They affect all industries and are especially critical for retailing. For example, the Wall Street Journal reported that Office Depot, a large U.S.-based office supply chain, got off to a rocky start in Japan because their aisles were too wide. Their stores had more appeal in Japan when aisles were narrow and crowded with products. This was how Japanese were used to buying in local stores. It was opposite to the 'open' concept, which is popular in the United States.

The use of color also needs to be carefully evaluated. A German company encountered this problem when marketing its products in Hong Kong. The company insisted on uniformity of packaging and literature. Because a brown color scheme worked well for them in Europe they wanted to use the same in Hong Kong. Their plans met resistance from the local Chinese manager who insisted that brown was considered a 'dirty' color and recommended white instead. White connotes purity and 'gives a good feeling.' Ultimately, the company had to adopt the white color scheme for Hong Kong and subsequently throughout Asia while keeping the brown version for Europe.

Other cultural factors to consider when marketing products are social values, gender roles, social stratification, and education. Social values involve attitudes related to tradition, status, and wealth as well as what is generally considered acceptable or non-acceptable in a society. Gender roles, including status and expectations, also vary across cultures. Definitions of masculinity and femininity from dress to behavior need to be considered, along with social stratifications.

Consequently, some products may be accepted in one form by one social segment but have to be changed to appeal to another segment.

Saatchi and Saatchi ran into problems with social and gender values when they started marketing Pamper disposable nappies (diapers) in Thailand. They promoted the fact that the nappies were convenient. This approach caused unexpected buying resistance from Thai women, who were worried that using disposable nappies would brand them as bad mothers more concerned about their own convenience than the babies' comfort. As a result, the company changed its approach to convince mothers that disposable nappies stay drier than cloth ones, making them more comfortable for the babies.

A key cultural variable in Asia is religion. Asia is home to many religions including Islam, Hinduism, Buddhism, Shintoism, and Christianity. One must be particularly careful when using symbols that can connote religious meaning or impressions.

Even an experienced global company like McDonald's can make serious mistakes. During a World Cup promotion, McDonald's printed the flags of 24 competitor countries on throwaway hamburger wrappers. One of the flags was the green and white flag of Saudi Arabia, which contains words sacred to Muslims. It is of course sacrilegious to use such words and symbols on commercial packaging, especially wrapping paper which will be soiled by food and then discarded. McDonald's offended Muslims around the world by inadvertently desecrating both the Saudi flag and the holy Koran. The promotion was quickly changed, but not before two million wrappers had already been printed.

A similar problem occurred in the 1990s, when photos of a famous German supermodel wearing a low-cut dress made by a well-known Italian designer appeared worldwide. Outraged Muslims pointed out that the bodice of the dress was covered with Arabic words from their holy book, the Koran. When Muslim leaders protested vehemently at the use of their sacred writings to promote a product, the Italian designer had to apologize and halt promotion of that particular garment. Careful research is required to avoid that kind of cross-cultural faux pas.

While good product planning is necessary for success in Asia, it must be complemented by an effective pricing strategy.

Pricing Decisions

Pricing methods vary domestically, internationally, and by industry. We can use cost-up methods to determine pricing, or discount from list or retail prices. One can also price based on acceptable margins, channel expectations, or how competitors price. Other choices include variable pricing based on local costs, exchange-rate adjustment or taxation, or flexible pricing based on value-added criteria.

Whatever your choice, the key to international pricing is to understand which variables influence the price and then to decide where prices should be set as well as how they should be negotiated. These items influence international pricing:

Product Positioning and Mix

Product Demands: Regional and local

Product Uniqueness: special features or a technological edge

Product Modification: costs related to market adaptation

Costs of Goods: manufacturing or production costs

Logistics Costs: transportation, shipping and handling

Sales Channel Expenses: distribution costs, levels of commission and expected channel profit levels

Import-Export Variables: taxes, duties and surcharges

Government Regulations: especially regarding transfer pricing

Currency Variations: inflation, monetary fluctuation, and exchange risks

Local Terms and Conditions: allowances, rebates, and discounts

Service Expectations: type of service, levels of service

Competitive Situation: extent of competition, positioning of competitors, competitive price levels, and anticipated competition

All of these factors influence pricing and vary between countries. But how a company approaches international pricing also has an impact. The foremost issue is how important Asia is relative to your strategy.

Also important is whether your company takes a centralized or decentralized approach to pricing decisions. Centralized pricing carries benefits in a globalized market where uniform pricing across markets may be necessary, driven by customer demand or competition with a global presence. Uniform prices in different markets also helps control gray-market activity. Some companies seek tight control over their corporate brands, a policy that is strengthened through centralized pricing. It can also benefit companies where production output heavily influences price. Ultimately, centralized pricing reflects the degree of control a company wants on its pricing process.

Decentralized pricing has advantages when your company's products and services vary widely from country to country, as can be the case in Asia. It allows for flexibility in local markets and consideration for different end-user characteristics such as income levels. Depending on how a company is organized, it can aid in the timing of pricing decisions. Decentralized pricing also allows greater sensitivity to local costs and conditions, including adaptation, and value-added requirements as well as variable costs related to local logistics, market entry, and sales channel needs.

However, most companies operating in Asia blend centralized pricing with decentralized pricing, or at least get local inputs to arrive at a focused corporate approach.

Another variable is transfer pricing, which takes place between entities of the same corporation. If your company has a subsidiary or joint venture in Asia and wants to sell through them, then some form of transfer pricing has to be established. This is among the most closely guarded secrets in many companies, because transfer-pricing formulas vary widely, impact competitiveness and corporate profitability, and carry tax implications. How a company sets its inter-company transfer prices influences how much money is paid in taxes to one country versus another. Though transfer pricing is carefully scrutinized by every country's tax authorities, it is necessary in order to transfer goods across borders.

Prices must be negotiated whether the product is being exported to Asia or is being sold from within the region. When negotiating price, these variables should be considered:

- Product demand
- Delivery requirements
- Local packaging needs
- Special paperwork including language or printing needs
- Currency requirements
- Import credits to offset exports
- Discounts, rebates, offsetting purchases
- Local inventory costs
- Product variations
- Perceived product value
- Sales volume

- Shipping costs
- Manufacturing or shipping locations
- Exchange rates
- Duties
- Delivery terms
- Payment terms

One of the biggest issues facing exporters in negotiating prices is exchange-rate risk – always a factor when dealing in more than one currency. The best way to avoid this is to sell only in your local currency. However, this option may not be available when there is strong local competition or if the buyer has sufficient leverage.

There are different ways to deal with this problem. Some exporters include an exchange-rate clause in their contracts so that if exchange rates change by a certain percentage over a given time period the exporter has the right to change prices. Others hedge by purchasing currency futures on the money market to protect against sudden fluctuations. Many exporters just rely on their Asian distributors to deal with the exchange risks, thereby buffering themselves from currency fluctuations.

It is obvious that products and pricing are key issues for selling in Asia. But good products and acceptable prices are still not enough. You have to get the products to market, and that entails having an effective entry strategy and good sales channels.

4. Exploring a Network
Market Entry: Basic Considerations

Good products, even when well adapted to the market and appropriately priced, are still not enough to guarantee success in Asia. If your product doesn't reach the customer in a cost-effective and locally acceptable manner, your attempts to develop business will be costly, troublesome, and likely futile. Therefore, market-entry and sales-channel selection need to be given careful thought.

Several market-entry considerations must be evaluated. These include the choice of markets – since deciding which market to access affects sales channel availability and selection. So market evaluation must be part of your research and planning process. Asian markets vary widely in economic development, ranging from established and highly developed markets such as Japan to emerging and less developed markets such as Vietnam. Some (e.g. Singapore) have excellent infrastructures while others have poor infrastructures, for example Cambodia.

Of course, even a socio-economically less developed country can be a good market for your product. For example, a manager who attended one of our University of Wisconsin seminars was successfully marketing bull semen in Asia for reproducing better strains of cattle. In this case, Korea was an established market while China was considered an emerging market with growth potential. Market selection and definition in this case were influenced by product potential.

Other important market-entry considerations include choice of location, resource needs, resource allocation, the timing of market entry, and partnering. Politically, some Asian governments find it more desirable for foreign companies to have a local partner, some even mandate local partnering as a condition for market participation. There are also competitive reasons for partnering, including the need for local resources or gaining the assets and competencies of Asian partners. Risk-sharing reasons include leveraging human resources, minimizing financial investments, or hedging against fast changing and potentially adverse conditions.

If you do decide to partner in the market, it is important that the partner you choose fit your organizational strategy. The following points should be discussed and agreed upon:

– Mutual motives; the partners should have common objectives
– Resource and asset contribution: what each side contributes
– Organizational structure and methods for measuring success
– Methods of control and determining how decisions will be made
– Communication needs, monitoring mechanisms, and levels of authority
– Cultural compatibility

Cultural compatibility between partners is particularly important and is often a problem for Asian and Western companies, since business practices may vary so greatly. The values and expectations of each party need to be clearly understood. Levels, needs, and methods of communication should be carefully analyzed, because misunderstandings and breakdowns in communication are among the most common problems in business partnerships. Most importantly, there needs to be mutual respect between partners, especially at the managerial level.

Once market-entry decisions have been made, the next issue is the selection of appropriate sales channels. There is usually a variety of sales channels to choose from: domestic export channels, direct sales to a foreign user, local foreign distribution, licensing, joint ventures, subsidiaries, and strategic alliances. Each channel has its merits and drawbacks.

Domestic Export Channels

The most common domestic export channels are foreign buying agents or offices, export resellers, export management companies, and domestic distributors.

1. Foreign buying agencies can be either government or private companies. In some cases, governments set up their own buying offices to procure materials or goods, normally focusing on commodities or natural resources. Some private companies also maintain procurement offices to source goods for their own needs. Japanese companies have pioneered this effort through International Procurement Offices, known as IPO's. The purpose of these

companies is to source materials and parts worldwide to provide better availability or pricing. Because of computerized technology, efficient organization, and effective logistics, such operations are becoming profit centers for many companies. Selling domestically to one of these organizations can be an effective way to get your product into the Asian market.

2. Export resellers are often found in the retail markets. They buy products which they repackage and sell in Asia. Often products are sold under different brand names or sometimes the reseller's own name. In some cases, the product may be sold under its original name but many need to be repackaged in order to adapt to the local market.

3. The most common domestic export channel is the export management company or EMC. You can use an EMC as a replacement for your own export department or as a supplement to other international sales channels. Normally, EMCs have relationships and methods that allow them to act as effective sales intermediaries. They usually handle a variety of different products. Some EMCs provide a distribution function, others only represent your products and channel them to the end customers.

The following example from the late 1990s illustrates the role played by export management companies in entering Asian markets.

Big Hammer Inc., a U.S. manufacturer of safety materials used in construction projects, had a very small export department focused mainly on Latin America. When research indicated that Japan had strong export potential, BHI management was interested but realized they didn't have the in-house resources required to tackle this big market on their own.

About that time, while visiting a local trade show BHI's export manager met representatives of Pacific Rim Exports, an export management company, and discussed Japan. After a couple of meetings to agree on the commission rate and other details, BHI and PRE signed a contract.

James Leslie, PRE's marketing manager, soon spotted an interesting Wall Street Journal ad placed by a large Japanese *keiretsu*, Nippon Kansai Construction Ltd. NKC was looking to source various products and services in North America. James answered the ad immediately on BHI's behalf, but based on experience expected to wait a while for a response from Japan. Sure enough, several months passed before PRE received a fax requesting a detailed proposal, including a pro forma invoice.

The two sides corresponded for well over a year. Then, almost two years after the initial contact, three senior NKC executives flew to the U.S. to discuss a possible purchase of BHI's patented safety materials. James arranged for two interpreters and worked out a precise, minute-by-minute itinerary for the three days the Japanese managers would be in town. He and his PRE colleagues met the NKC delegation at the airport, took them to lunch and then sightseeing.

The next morning the group toured the Big Hammer factory, went out for lunch and then sat down for a four-hour negotiation. James could see from the tenor of the discussions that agreement was highly likely. After gifts and pleasantries were exchanged, the PRE team drove the Japanese back to their hotel to get ready for an elegant dinner hosted by BHI's top management. The next day James and his team accompanied the Japanese visitors to the airport and said their goodbyes.

There followed six more months of almost daily correspondence about specifications, quality standards and product adaptation plus Japan visits by James Leslie. Finally NKC did place a large order and opened a letter of credit. Big Hammer's product line was now launched in Japan.

This case shows why manufacturers both large and small choose an export management company to handle all or some specific overseas markets. Big Hammer didn't have the experience and know-how to crack the Japan market; Pacific Rim Exports did. PRE was willing to work on a commission basis, so Big Hammer incurred no cost unless they made a sale. Like many other export management companies, PRE also bought goods from domestic manufacturers for resale abroad, but BHI preferred the commission arrangement.

Many contracts with EMCs stipulate that when export sales to a given market reach a certain level, the manufacturer has the option to take over specified markets itself. So it is possible to use an export management company to test the waters, so to speak. Then, if that market-entry strategy works, the manufacturer can build up its own export department to run the business.

The case also illustrates some of the complexities involved in cracking Asian markets. PRE's Japan marketing campaign took over two and a half years from the initial contact to the first shipment. Which shows once again that doing business in Asia takes patience, hard work and market-specific expertise.

4. Globally expanding domestic distributors such as Arrow, Future, and Avnet have found that in order to grow their business, they have to establish themselves overseas. Those that expand to Asia often pull their existing U.S. or European suppliers with them into Asia, or they may seek new suppliers better suited to the Asian region. If such a distributor has sufficient leverage, it may be able to force suppliers to develop an international focus.

Of course, such a move can cause channel conflicts if you already have local distributors in Asia. Issues such as differential pricing between markets, product variations, and customer service/support may need to be addressed. Channel conflicts revolving around territories or assigned customers can become serious problems. Essentially, multiple-country distributors are hybrid organizations that service domestic as well as foreign needs. They usually operate independently from the control of any one supplier, so it's important to carefully weigh the pros and cons of this channel strategy.

The main benefits of using domestic export sales channels are the ease of doing business and lower marketing costs. Servicing these organizations requires less effort than other vehicles, but on the other hand, you will probably have little market visibility and less control over the way your product is marketed.

Direct Sales to Foreign Buyers: The E-Business Option

Direct sales to end-users in Asia is another form of export channeling. However, this is the least common and most specialized form of selling, normally reserved for foreign government procurement requirements or for companies needing unique materials, services, or information. Direct selling requires direct relationships and communication, which need to be established and actively managed.

A new and growing form of this type of export channel involves e-business. With the development of computerized communications and the Net, some companies are developing direct-marketing programs for sales to Asia, aided by enhanced electronics communication and information flow. This form of marketing may not totally supplant interpersonal relationships and traditional local sales channels but can help initiate contacts for later direct sales opportunities. It can also be used in conjunction with existing sales channels in the region, such as direct exports.

Littelfuse, for example, established FUSE 119 in Japan. This is an effective Net service for promoting their fuse products and help customers with application issues. In Japan, 119 is a common emergency number like 911 is in the United States. Customers e-mail this number to make inquiries or seek solutions requiring Littelfuse products. The end result may be a direct sale, or it may be a step towards a customer relationship which can lead to new or further business.

E-business continues to grow in Asia. The Japanese average more days per month online than residents of any other country, and are second only to Americans in Web usage. Other Asian countries, including China, find e-commerce an effective way to develop contacts and conduct transactions. Virtually any market in Asia can now be accessed via the Net.

The efficiency and cost benefits of information technology challenge traditional sales channels and methods of conducting business. In Japan, for example, some consumers prefer to buy over the Web, citing the savings in time, money, and reduced stress as reasons. Innovative companies have responded and one now sells automobiles through the Internet. E-business sales, however, are still relatively small in Japan and require strategies tailored to specific consumer interests and tastes.

Industrial and commercial procurement needs help pave the way for e-commerce; efficiency and cost effectiveness are leading motivators. NEC, a large Japanese manufacturer, utilizes an Internet-based procurement system which globally accesses nearly 6,500 parts suppliers. NEC's goal is to shorten lead times, obtain price advantages, and better respond to demand changes – all of which help reduce total business costs.

Likewise, Raffles Holdings Ltd., a hotel and hospitality group, is pioneering e-procurement in Singapore to achieve cost targets, reduce inventories, and effectively access suppliers. Raffles procures all types of products in this manner, reducing its supplier base to a select, cost-effective group. In China, General Electric started using e-auctions to get price quotations from potential suppliers, resulting in significant savings through reduced prices even though the distribution inefficiencies common to China raised delivery costs.

In Asia, many companies are exploring e-procurement as a way to better manage their supply chain, improve operating efficiencies, and enhance competitiveness. As a result, export marketers may need to consider and incorporate e-business solutions in order to effectively meet the needs of their customers and maintain competitiveness. But this should be done carefully, since e-business does not eliminate the cultural barriers to doing business in Asia. If anything, it can even make things more challenging. The question is how well companies will be able to assimilate e-commerce into the local culturally-determined ways of doing business. Success will require ingenuity, cultural sensitivity, and managerial effectiveness.

If a company decides to use e-commerce, it is important to understand how different Asian countries regulate online information and products. Just as there are rules, barriers, and limitations affecting the physical marketing of products, there are also rules, barriers, and limitations affecting the electronic marketing of products (and services). All major Asian countries have laws regulating e-commerce, so before pursuing such a program we suggest researching local laws. Violations can attract fines or even imprisonment. Key areas of compliance include:

Marketing Techniques and Standards: Regulations may restrict or outlaw certain promotional methods such as lotteries, sweepstakes, games of chance, free gifts, certain discounts or similar online incentives. Some regulations restrict advertising. The Philippines, for example, requires advertising material to comply with an Advertising Board ethical code. Taiwan and Thailand have similar compliance codes.

Consumer Protection: Regulations aimed at false, unacceptable, or misleading information including fraud, deceptive practices, illicit contracts, certain rebates, or other unsanctioned activities. Often, they focus on governing 'distant selling' to conform to local acceptance and practice. Japan, for example, has direct-selling laws that regulate warranties, pricing, delivery practices and other such issues. Likewise, South Korean laws regulate telemarketing and multilevel selling.

Content Restrictions: Regulations restrict information considered socially unacceptable such as political, religious, ethical, cultural, or sexual content. China, for example, has particularly complicated rules regarding such issues, requiring state-approved sources and compliance with anti-subversion laws. Even news distribution on the Web can be highly scrutinized and subject to various limitations. In addition, content restriction laws in some countries may be implicit and vague, based on cultural expectations or even political necessity – making it difficult to know exactly what is restricted.

Privacy: Laws protecting personal information collected via the Web, such as e-mail addresses, credit card numbers, names, and personal or financial information.

In addition to laws regulating business on the Web, there may also be restrictions as to what types of businesses can use e-commerce. For example, gambling and the sale of pharmaceuticals may be restricted or outlawed altogether. Banking, securities, and insurance may be subject to special regulations, while legal, medical, or financial services often require a license.

Distribution and Local Asian Sales Channels

The most popular method of entry into the Asian market is via Asian sales channels. Most Western marketers choose them as their primary sales vehicle; others select them as supplemental vehicles. The most common types include Asian sales representatives, agents, retailers, trading companies, and distributors.

Sales Representatives

Sales representatives are individuals or companies engaged in the sale of products. Most Asian sales reps work on commission or some other agreed-upon compensation plan. They often represent a number of different suppliers and leverage multi-product selling into their value for both suppliers and customers. Usually, representatives specialize in certain products or markets. Since true sales reps are substitutes for your firm's own in-house sales force, they require a company to be involved with the direct export of goods to customers.

In some cases, local Asian sales representatives are used in conjunction with local distributors to sell products, and may even manage the local distributor's efforts. In other cases, Asian representatives provide a distribution function for some product lines by importing, inventorying, and distributing products themselves.

Agents

In Asia the functions of an agent and a sales representative are so similar that the terms are often used interchangeably. However, we should be very careful when using the term 'agent' in contracts, correspondence, or designation, because some Asian countries consider 'agents' legal representatives or extensions of a foreign company with the authority to bind a company to decisions or transactions. If the terms 'agent' or 'agency' are used in your agreements, be sure to get good legal advice specific to your Asian market.

Local Retailers

Asian retailers are primarily found in consumer markets and may in some cases buy and import directly from foreign suppliers. Normally, larger retailers fit into this category because they have a warehouse function and redistribute to their own outlets. However, most Asian retailers buy through distributors or trading companies specialized in certain goods, through which the retailer can combine purchases. In some cases, such as in Japan, there may be secondary or even tertiary distributors (wholesalers) in the channel before goods ultimately reach the retail level. Such complex systems represent a non-tariff trade barrier for exporters trying to access the Japanese markets.

Trading Companies

Most trading companies are large corporations engaged in the import, distribution, and export of products. Trading companies in Asia can be private, public, or even government-controlled. State-controlled trading companies normally focus on sensitive raw materials, agriculture, specialized technologies, aerospace, or military equipment, while commercial trading companies handle just about anything.

While some trading companies are small and specialized, most are large organizations involved in banking, real estate, insurance, transportation and sometimes manufacturing. Because of their size, connections, and influence, trading companies can be good vehicles for market entry. In Japan, for example, twenty-nine trading companies control the majority of the country's imports and exports. The ten largest control over half of Japan's imports and exports as well as nearly twenty percent of the wholesale trade. Thus, working with one of these companies may be a good tactic.

In some industries, large companies may even have their own in-house trading companies to help make it easier to access smaller suppliers. In Japan, Toyota and Matsushita have such operations.

Controlling a large trading company as your export sales channel can be a daunting task, however. This is particularly true if your product line is not of substantial benefit, does not generate significant revenue, or is not of particular importance to the trading company.

Distributors

Another common market-entry mode for Asia involves specialized or general distributors. Like reps or agents, Asian distributors may focus on specific markets, single countries, multiple countries, or the region as a whole. They may also appear under different labels, such as wholesalers, agents, stocking representatives, retail suppliers, value-added retailers, value-added dealers, importers, trading companies, resellers, management companies, jobbers, stockists, and others. Names may vary, but they all refer to distributors.

For our purpose, a distributor is any firm functioning as a distributor, i.e. a service organization focused on market needs. Its main benefit to both the manufacturer and the customer is that it absorbs a number of costs involved with doing business. From the manufacturer's standpoint, benefits are:

- Carrying inventory required to service the needs of the customer
- Handling scheduled orders
- Selling and promoting
- Carrying receivables and whatever credit losses may occur

From the Asian customer's standpoint they are:
- Carrying inventory required to run the customer's business
- Ordering flexibility
- Service and delivery
- Extending credit
- Single-source convenience for procuring multiple products.

Additional services an Asian distributor may provide:
- Handling currency risk
- Providing communication and translation expertise
- Enhancing relationships and local knowledge
- Providing resources for cultural adaptation such as repackaging or re-labeling products, creating or translating literature to local needs, or modifying products or services to meet local requirements.

Many Asian distributors enhance their services through the Internet and electronic data interchanges (EDI). Some provide technical and application support through product specialists and engineers. Others focus on supply-chain management including enhanced communications, just-in-time delivery, ship-to-stock programs, quality assurance agreements, and other value-added capabilities.

An Asian distributor's key strength lies in its market focus: a combination of its sales orientation, choice of customers, services, and its major product lines. Depending on the country, or territories within countries, one or more distributors may be needed.

In order to maximize market focus through distribution, you should avoid having too many distributors concentrating on the same market or customer base. Normally with networks of multiple distributors, there will be some market overlap. However, the key to Asian market expansion is to obtain and align distributors so as to minimize overlap and maximize coverage. The end result will be greater market penetration and sales potential.

It is important to align the strengths and focus of the exporter/ supplier with those of the distributor. In Asia, this is easier said than done. Some countries, particularly developing ones, have fewer markets and distributors, so we employ simple distribution systems. Others have more sophisticated and complex structures: Japan, for example, boasts distribution systems that go back centuries.

Accessing customers may require using multiple distribution systems involving a series of sub-distributors before goods reach the consumer level. This tends to be true in the more relationship-oriented Asian cultures. Structuring a distribution network gets complicated if you are not familiar with the business styles of your particular markets.

Developing an effective distribution network in Asia raises issues such as getting share of mind, supporting distributor activities, and monitoring and measuring distributor performance. However, the first task for many companies is simply to locate good distributors. Here are some proven ways:

– Get recommendations from your customers or end-users in Asia.
– Find out which distributors your current customers prefer.
– Read industrial publications, trade journals and magazines.
– Contact your government's embassies, foreign commercial offices or distributor referral services.
– Take advantage of industry- or government-sponsored trade missions and 'matchmaking' tours.

- Attend world-trade group meetings in your area.
- Tap industry councils in your country.
- Contact industry associations in your Asian target markets.
- Use trade-development organizations for target countries, e.g. JETRO in Japan.
- Ask manufacturers in target countries.
- Get referrals from suppliers of related products or services already doing business in Asia.
- See what your sister company or other divisions use.
- Attend foreign and domestic trade shows.
- Contact foreign embassies and/or consulates.
- Hire consultants who know about distribution in the area.
- Use your state, local, or provincial export assistance centers.
- Network with local distributors and your international connections.
- Use distributor councils and associations.
- Find out which distributors the suppliers or manufacturers of complementary products use.
- Determine which distributors your competitors are using.
- Check out domestic and international online sites.
- Look for ads in local newspapers or magazines.
- Contact universities, colleges, trade schools, and business schools (local and Asian).
- Use libraries.
- Hire research firms.
- Thumb through the local telephone directory when visiting your Asian markets.

You will need to network and establish a database. List the key assets and capabilities you desire in a distributor and set up a spreadsheet to help you assess them. This will aid decision-making and help provide an objective analysis. First-hand input also aids comprehension and provides sensitivity in the research process. In other words, sometimes you need to just get on a plane and go over there to take a look around.

China is a case in point. Industries used to be told what to make and where to sell their goods. This was simple until the country opened and began integrating its markets with foreign corporations. Competition developed and new markets emerged, but the development of sales and distribution channels did not keep pace.

For many industries such channels simply did not exist. Companies such as Littlefuse had to innovate in order to develop channels. Because of China's expanding manufacturing base, Littelfuse saw a need for its fuse products but discovered that there were no traditional channels of distribution. So here was a booming market with no established means of access!

As a first step, Littelfuse decided to develop name recognition and contacts through trade shows. During one such show, a Chinese gentleman speaking the Shanghainese dialect approached the company's representatives. He examined the products closely and said, 'I can sell this product. So when can I start?'

The man's name was Charles, owner of a small business in Shanghai who was looking for new business opportunities. Charles didn't know much about fuses, but believed that because China was developing electronics manufacturing, it would need such parts. Charles figured that he was just the guy to do it if he could get in early and develop a network. None of their other leads produced promising, so Littelfuse decided to give him a chance.

'Shanghai Charles' was off and running. Focusing on his native region, he studied potential customers and market trends, diligently followed up on leads and contacts, and networked with associates and friends to foster relationships. Selling in China requires 'guanxi': a network of personal relationships. Soon sales flourished and Shanghai Charles became one of Littelfuse's leading sales agents and an expert in his field.

When faced with the lack of sales channels in Asian, you may need to innovate. Creating your own distribution system can be an alternative when no viable channels are available – or when traditional channels are blocked by competition.

Another major distribution issue in Asia is the question of exclusivity. Whether or not to have an exclusive distributor is one of the most important points to decide when organizing a distribution network in the Pacific Rim. It is an issue not only when the network is being established, but also when market changes require a realignment of distributors.

The advantage of having exclusivity is greater 'share of mind'. You can channel all your sales and support through a single distributor, thus maximizing attention and efforts to expand sales. You may also use exclusivity to keep competitors from using the same distributor. Exclusivity also enables you to fully support your distributor's business and helps offset his start-up costs when developing the business.

For the Asian distributor, of course, exclusivity also helps tie up a supplier and gives the distributor more control over the business.

The disadvantage of an exclusive arrangement is that it limits the flexibility of both supplier and distributor. The distributor may be unable to access better suppliers should business conditions change, and is dependent on the performance of the supplier for support through products and services. If the supplier cannot perform competitively, then the distributor's business will suffer. Likewise, an exclusive arrangement may prevent the supplier from finding better distributors in the event of changing business conditions. If a distributor is marketing to the wrong customer base or otherwise not making the best use of the supplier's potential, success will be difficult.

For some exporters, the exclusivity issue is not important. Some companies are happy to have just about any distributor for certain locations in Asia, whether exclusive or not. On the other hand, cultural factors may necessitate exclusivity. In Japan, for example, many customers prefer to have their supplier select the distributor they are to use, in effect making distributors exclusive for them.

In Asia exclusivity arrangements can take different forms. You can negotiate them for an individual country or for multiple countries, by region or territory, by customer or customer groups, by markets, products, or product groups – even by technology. You can also have multiple distributors within one country, each with exclusivity over certain customers, markets, products, or technologies.

You might also have an exclusive distributor handling not only Japanese companies in Japan but also Japanese transplant customers throughout Asia. You might take that route for cultural, communication, or account coordination reasons.

Changing market trends can also impact exclusivity arrangements. When your home-country distributors relocate to Asia, they will likely try to sell the lines they are currently carrying. They may do this on their own or ask to be franchised, which can cause conflicts if you already have existing exclusivity arrangements in Asia. Finally there is the problem of 'parallel imports'. That's where one of your home-country distributors begins to export your product to Asian markets in which you already have an exclusivity agreement. This situation, increasingly common, causes major sales-channel disruption and contractual disputes.

A major key to marketing success in Asia is finding the right distributors and structuring a network to maximize market penetration.

Because of the scope and size of the Asian region, many companies take a targeted approach by adding distributors in a manner that best utilizes available resources.

The targeted approach for example involves setting up distributors based on realistic sales potential as well as on your company's ability to support the needs of those distributors. Some exporters try to deploy a number of distributors at once in order to facilitate quick coverage in many different countries.

The danger in that approach is that since not all markets develop at the same speed, sales may not be sufficient to support a broad distributor base. A better solution is to selectively add distributors one by one, based on sales potential and available resources. The worst thing you can do is to employ distributors you cannot support.

Particularly in Asia, your relationships with distributors are critical and must be continually cultivated in order to enhance business.

It is important to get all distribution agreements in writing. This not only helps affirm commitments, it also allows for the protection of mutual rights in the event of changing business conditions or possible termination of the distribution arrangement. We will look at rules for negotiating effective distribution agreements a bit further along.

Licensing and Franchising: Pros and Cons

Licensing is another popular market-entry method for Asia. Licensing means assigning the rights of something to another company in exchange for some reciprocal right or compensation. Normally this involves assigning an Asian company the right to manufacture, sell or use a product, provide a specified or guaranteed service, or utilize software or some other media under specific terms or limitations.

Some benefits of licensing are:

1. Minimal capital outlay required – particularly beneficial when your resources are limited.
2. A possible supplement to exporting – especially when an Asian manufacturing presence is needed.
3. A way to overcome import restrictions such as tariff and non-tariff barriers.
4. Useful in countries sensitive to foreign ownership – particularly where local law limits or prevents foreign equity investment.
5. Protection of patents and trademarks from non-use cancellation.

6. Provides a steady stream of revenue – generally for a specified period of time.

The drawbacks:
1. Often less profitable than other vehicles. Payment levels, terms and duration of the license are often hotly negotiated.
2. Provides no market control. You can easily license away your freedom of action as well as prospects for growth and diversity in given markets. This drawback has victimized many companies particularly during their early growth stage in Asia.
3. Could possibly create a competitor. Giving technical know-how to an Asian company may nurture a future business adversary. This has happened to many unsuspecting companies which have entered license agreements. Your global competitiveness can be harmed instead of enhanced.

With all this in mind, marketers must carefully weigh licensing as a possible strategy for Asia. The prospect of creating a competitor that could some day sell into the licensor's domestic market merits special attention. This threat has steered many companies away from license agreements.

Still, numerous exporters have incorporated licensing into their Asian strategy. Some use it in conjunction with other market vehicles – licensing certain products but retaining others for direct marketing. Other companies take different approaches. One firm, for example, licenses goods nearing the end of their product life cycles. Others license products for manufacture under a different name in order to avoid market conflicts and to protect the integrity of their brand name.

Still others license products for manufacture with the stipulation that all goods are sold to the licensee, thereby neatly controlling both sales channel and price levels.

In licensing arrangements, as in other Asian business relationships, knowing the company you are doing business with and understanding their motives and desires are of utmost importance. Such knowledge and understanding require building a strong relationship and managing it. Mutual understanding goes a long way in avoiding problems and solving conflicts as they arise. However, since license arrangements can more easily become arms-length deals than other types of entry modes, it is good to include in your agreement levels of control that can help maintain your business objectives. This should be done in conjunction with good legal counsel, since what is lawful or unlawful varies by country.

Licenses are usually based on patents or know-how and are for the manufacture, use, or sale of a product or products. Various methods of control can be considered. You might stipulate time limits along with restrictions on territory and the use of know-how. Where possible, you might prohibit the licensee from handling competitive products or selling the same or similar products to competitors. Substituting products might also be prohibited. You could also stipulate that information and know-how regarding the license cannot be disclosed to other parties. Also consider a clause protecting your trade names, trademarks, or other intellectual property.

You may wish to add other clauses to license arrangements that:

1. Set a minimum quantity on what is manufactured, sold, or used.
2. Require a guaranteed level of quality in the manufacture of licensed products.
3. Stipulate disclosure of amount manufactured and/or sold, for royalty purposes. This also helps monitor the licensee.
4. Extend the license agreement in such a way as to require royalty payments (also known as deferred payments) even after the expiration of a patent.
5. Require the licensee to inform the licensor of any knowledge or know-how acquired in conjunction with utilizing the licensed technology.
6. Stipulate disclosure regarding improvements acquired through the use of the license that may even include a provision granting the licensor rights to such improvements.
7. Restrict the export of licensed products or products acquired by licensed know-how by territory, price, and/or quantity; or require exports to be sold through the licensor only.
8. Limit the level of technology transferred in the agreement.
9. Require the licensee to purchase certain parts, materials, assemblies or related goods from the licensor or suppliers designated by the licensor. This is a good way to ensure the quality of the licensed product.

Licensing can be effective in markets where other modes of entry are difficult. For example, Ace Hardware, a large U.S.-based retailer, used licensing to enter Japan's mature home-improvement market. Research showed that a considerable market existed in Japan for their type of operation. Although the country had close to 3,500 home centers and 19,000 hardware stores, none fit the style of business Ace wanted to introduce to Japan.

For nearly ten years, Ace sought ways to penetrate the market, including negotiating with large trading companies, distributors, and home-center chains. Management determined that exporting through these channels would be too costly and would not allow the kind of program needed to be successful in the market. As a result, the company decided the best vehicle would be to partner with a local company through a license agreement. Ace's partner would pay a license fee and royalties as well as be required to purchase a certain percentage of their inventory from Ace. The U.S. firm would provide know-how including store design and layout support. In this case, Ace used licensing to overcome barriers presented by more traditional entry modes in Japan [National Home Center News, December 11, 2000]. Elsewhere in Asia Ace has used franchises, dealers, or Ace-affiliated stores to access markets.

Franchising, another form of licensing, is also becoming popular in Asia, especially among retailers, service providers, and food outlets such as McDonald's and Kentucky Fried Chicken. It can be considered a partnership arrangement, a notion that helped American restaurant chain TGI Friday succeed in Asia. Franchisees not only helped set up and run the business in the prescribed style, they also helped navigate local hurdles such as red tape, labor unions, and hiring practices.

Joint Ventures: Pros and Cons

The joint venture is another mode of market entry via a partnership arrangement. A JV can be defined as an association of two or more parties to achieve a common business objective. Each party contributes certain resources and, depending on what is contributed, usually assumes a share of the risks and rewards resulting from the undertaking. Ownership is shared in defined portions usually on a percentage basis.

Joint ventures take many forms. They can be created for sales and distribution, manufacturing, service, or resource development. A joint venture can be formed by acquiring a percentage of an existing company or by two or more companies creating a new entity through joint investment. Joint ventures have both benefits and drawbacks, which should be considered before pursuing this option in Asia.

The benefits:
1. Reduce the political and economic risks of market entry
2. Enable an exporter to tap into the special skills, know-how, and resources of a local Asian partner
3. Allow access to Asian markets and distribution systems otherwise not accessible
4. Reduce capital outlays and start-up expenses
5. Offer tax advantages (depending on the country)
6. Share management burdens

The drawbacks:
1. Rewards (profits) must be shared
2. Reduce freedom of action in decision making
3. Restrict ownership
4. Partners frequently disagree regarding goals, direction, or vision
5. Shared management complicates decision-making and problem solving.

Because of partnership issues, joint ventures can be complicated and are often compared to marriages. Like a good marriage, the bond and strength of the partnership can lead to success and an enduring relationship. However, if the partnership is riddled with obstacles that cannot be overcome or negotiated, then living with such an arrangement can be a nightmare. Breaking up a joint venture can be as traumatic and unsettling as any divorce. In Asia, the management of joint ventures is further complicated by major culture and communication issues. And if a joint venture involves a Western company participating in Asia, then geographic distance complicates matters as well.

The key to a successful joint venture is knowing what you are getting into up front. Right from the start you must assess and understand your partner's goals, aspirations, and capabilities. It is important to determine each other's requirements, risk tolerance, expectations and the value of each side's contribution, as well as to define markets and territories and decide how the joint venture is to be controlled.

The wise manager addresses the following issues when contemplating a joint venture:

- Percentage of ownership
- Degree of control, especially in terms of the management structure and board of directors
- How directors or officers are chosen, or replaced if one resigns
- How shares are transferred
- Resolution of deadlocks
- Termination procedures, notice and the distribution of assets
- Supporting agreements or contracts such as those related to manufacturing or supply, compensation, non-competition, sales and distribution, employment, property or leases, licenses regarding intellectual property or new inventions

Most of the above items become part of a joint venture agreement, but you should consider them before entering into a JV in the first place. In Asia, what is of greatest concern to most companies is how to control a joint venture. The best way to do that is to find the right local partner and to communicate frequently. Joint ventures, like most relationships, need ongoing communication to deal with issues and solve problems. They are created and maintained through continuous negotiations.

In 50-50 joint ventures, here are six additional ways to exercise control:

1. Obtain the majority of director positions in the company
2. Stipulate that your directors will appoint management
3. Arrange the joint venture with a partner that has no interest in management
4. In case of a deadlock, arrange for tie votes to be decided by your directors
5. Issue voting and non-voting stock that can divide profits evenly between partners but will allow majority votes to your side.
6. Negotiate a lesser percentage of ownership between each partner, for example 40-40. Then place the remaining shares with a third partner favorable toward your position.

The above suggestions hold true for joint ventures with both manufacturing and sales responsibilities, by far the most common form of JV in Asia. However, some companies have taken the approach of dividing sales and manufacturing responsibilities for either control, market, investment, or resource needs. To accomplish this you create two or more joint ventures with the different operations having either sales or manufacturing responsibilities. One partner has majority ownership in the manufacturing venture, the other partner majority ownership in the sales venture. Ownership then depends on each partner's primary goals, interest and skill sets. Revenue sharing depends on percentage of ownership. One party makes more money on manufacturing, the other on sales.

One leading semiconductor manufacturer took this approach with some of its operations in Asia. Because of the high investment costs involved with semiconductor production, the company encouraged manufacturing joint ventures in which their partners would have majority shares. This reduced the company's financial risk and exposure, particularly during times of market volatility, common in that industry. However, the firm required that the joint venture's production go through their own sales channels, which allowed control over sales and helped compensate the company for being the minority shareholder in the manufacturing joint ventures.

For Western companies contemplating joint ventures in Asia and not wanting a complicated structure, the best way to develop and control a joint venture is to simply retain majority ownership. Even so, local laws governing joint venture ownership should be carefully studied. In some countries, majority ownership may not guarantee management control. For example, in Korea a 66.6% ownership or 'super majority' is needed for unilateral decision making.

Even with majority ownership, a JV can fail if management does not consider local culture and business style in the running of the operation. Some companies approach joint ventures as a takeover rather than as a partnership in a foreign land. The majority owner may try to impose its own culture or business style on the venture without considering local needs or the impact on business. This breeds mistrust and discontent, which will ultimately lead to a failed venture.

Subsidiaries: When to Go It Alone

For some companies, neither JVs nor exporting to distributors may be the best market-entry mode. In such cases, establishing a subsidiary or another such direct operation can be advantageous. Direct operations can be used to access resources and markets. They may focus on marketing and sales, manufacturing, service and support, engineering, procurement, or research and development. They can also be used to coordinate or manage distribution in the region. Like other forms of market entry, direct operations have both benefits and drawbacks which need to be carefully assessed.

The benefits:
1. Majority ownership, up to 100%
2. Greater control over activities
3. More freedom of action and decision-making
4. More likely to conform to your company's goals and objectives
5. No partnership risks. Can reduce conflicts of interests
6. Shows market commitment in countries such as Japan, Korea, and China
7. Opens up sales opportunities that may not be available to foreign importers because of local buying preferences or content requirements
8. May reduce manufacturing costs and certain tax burdens

The drawbacks:
1. A subsidiary generally requires greater capital commitment compared to other entry vehicles. Capital placed abroad is also subject to risk
2. Requires a larger management effort
3. Requires a lot of time and energy to establish and maintain operations
4. Often takes longer to achieve market entry
5. May not replace the need for other entry modes such as local distributors
6. As a foreign entity it can be subject to regulations such as local-content requirements, price controls and foreign-exchange controls.
7. Subject to economic risks such as inflation and currency-exchange fluctuations which can influence reported earnings

Some of the issues mentioned above affect some joint ventures as well. However, direct operations are generally more exposed to risks stemming from anti-foreign feelings such as legislation, strikes, demonstrations, union activities, or other such disturbances. The upside is that local subsidiaries are treated as local companies and thus may also receive government benefits and incentives such as tax holidays, rebates, financial assistance, special employment considerations, duty drawbacks or exemptions, and other favors.

The benefits to Asian countries of having direct investments through corporate subsidiaries or joint ventures are so great that many governments have their own inward-investment organizations. These also aid in developing contacts and relationships and in some cases help find local investors. Some investment promotion organizations even help with infrastructure development and obtaining resources or real estate.

Because setting up a subsidiary or other direct operation in Asia can be difficult, using government or private agencies or consultants to acquire local expertise is often a good idea. It may take a long time to get things done without local assistance. Some companies involve local silent partners for this very reason.

The different ways a foreign company can set up a direct operation in Asia include a representative office, branch office, or subsidiary. The choice of enterprise depends on a company's goals or strategy. A representative office (sometimes called 'liaison office') is not involved in sales and is fairly easy to establish. Functions are usually limited to the collection of information, research, or promotion and/or advertising. Such offices are carefully scrutinized by local governments to ensure that no sales activity takes place, as this would have local tax implications. Representative offices are easy to disband if there is a change in corporate focus.

Branch offices are extensions of the parent company and may perform sales activities as well as other types of functions such as engineering or research and development. The profit and loss of the branch is normally added to that of the head office. Usually, branch offices offer limited flexibility in tax strategy and are not considered separate legal entities from the parent company. If the branch is involved in a legal dispute, it affects the parent company, thereby putting assets at risk.

Subsidiaries are common direct-investment vehicles in Asia and are normally chosen for their ease of doing business as well as flexibility for tax and legal reasons. They can be structured in different ways to provide for any type of business function or enterprise and are not limited in scope as are representative offices or branch offices. Subsidiaries are often preferred by Asian governments as a direct-investment enterprise, as are joint ventures. Being a separate legal entity and essentially classified as a local company, the subsidiary has considerable independence. For example, if the subsidiary is involved in a legal dispute it will not jeopardize the corporate assets of the parent company.

In Asia it is necessary to get formal government approval to set up a subsidiary. Certain commitments will likely be required. Regulations governing foreign investment should be carefully reviewed and continually assessed since they may change frequently, depending on the country. Remember that subsidiaries are regulated by local laws, so it's vital to seek competent legal counsel when forming such an operation.

Subsidiaries can be established as a start-up or through a local acquisition. Start-ups require more initial resources and considerable commitment, as you are essentially building a new company. Start-ups may be preferred in Asia because you can mold the entity around your company's goals and focus it for success. However, these operations also take longer to establish. Local expertise is normally needed to shorten the learning curve and achieve success. Consequently, hiring qualified local staff is a critical element for start-ups.

Acquiring a local company is another way to establish a subsidiary in Asia. The object is to buy not just a facility but also to acquire know-how, expertise and possibly an existing channel to the market. Problems include timing, finding the right acquisition candidate, financial and facility issues, and a number of human resource concerns. Just as local Asian staff can be a benefit in making an acquisition, they can also be a drawback if the business cultures of the parent company and the acquisition are too different or incompatible. In some cases, local laws limit or restrict personnel changes, layoffs, and termination. Such restrictions can impede any restructuring effort.

If you choose the acquisition route, there are various ways to proceed. Most companies purchase only the assets of the acquired company, which helps avoid hidden liabilities. Others purchase newly issued or outstanding shares through a tender offer, or attempt a merger. Mergers need to be evaluated carefully in Asia because some countries may have laws preventing foreign companies from merging with local ones. In such cases, you might consider the strategy of first establishing a local subsidiary, then merging the subsidiary with the local acquisition.

Regardless of how a subsidiary is set up, it must still be managed. Although a subsidiary offers better control over management as well as flexibility in structure and direction, it does not eliminate the cultural factors that influence local business style and human behavior. Even when a company is directly owned, it still operates within a different culture. We must be sensitive to local business habits, social traditions, and the perspectives of local management. Continuous communication with the subsidiary is vital.

One common misconception regarding subsidiaries is that it is easier to deal with 'our own people.' In some cases this may be true, but not always. Subsidiary operations need active interface and communication with headquarters. That requires two-way communication and understanding. Having a subsidiary does not reduce the need for negotiation; it simply adds another dimension to it.

Strategic Alliances

The strategic alliance is another form of business partnership in Asia. Firms form strategic alliances to avail themselves of talent, know-how, technologies, resources or assets they do not have. Strategic alliances can take forms ranging from traditional manufacturing, sales or product development joint ventures to cooperative arrangements for product enhancements, sharing know-how, or cross licensing. They may also entail product swaps or complimentary sales endeavors, or can be a technology alliance aimed at the mutual development of new materials or products. Such joint-development programs can help you rapidly build competitive advantage. Strategic alliances are also set up to offer joint, cooperative, or complementary services.

In other words, strategic alliances can be almost anything from traditional joint ventures to creative partnering, depending on the attitudes and goals of the participants and the mutual benefits they hope to reap. These of course vary company by company as well as industry by industry.

In Asia even traditional production relationships such as contract manufacturing are now viewed as strategic alliances. This is particularly true when a high level of technology, resources, commitment and cooperation is required. Contract manufacturers specialize in making products for other companies, often under the latter's brand name. It is a popular form of production in Asia because many companies find it more cost effective to use contract manufacturers there than having their own manufacturing facilities.

In some cases, contract manufacturers supplement manufacturing done by corporate subsidiaries or joint ventures by providing logistics and procurement or related supply-chain management services. They will need to meet designated quality and time-to-market expectations. Such contractual relationships are sometimes considered strategic partnerships and managed as such. Confidentiality and trust become key components in the alliance.

Another form of strategic alliance in Asia is the partnering of manufacturing companies with logistics and transportation firms. Moving goods around Asia can be a daunting task, so having a logistical edge can provide a competitive advantage. Many companies move to Asia in order to gain manufacturing and marketing cost advantages only to see profits evaporate as they try to get products to market. Logistics can be a critical issue not just between countries but within countries as well. This is particularly true of China, with its vast expanses, huge bureaucracy and infrastructure limitations. Smaller countries like Thailand also present a logistical challenge when vendors want goods sold in every small town. The solution often lies in forming a strategic partnership with a firm that has an established logistics network.

Companies pursue strategic alliances for the same reasons they pursue other entry vehicles: to gain access to markets or technologies; to leverage resources they don't have or develop economies of scale; to expedite market entry or overcome barriers to entry; to share financial and other risks.

There are drawbacks to strategic alliances, however. They include possible confusion over objectives, direction, control, and decision-making. Lack of a common focus leads to a disjointed approach. Differences in resource contributions and levels of commitment can also be problematic. More importantly, if strategic requirements change, then the relationship itself will likely need to change.

Keeping the lines of communication open will enable partners to address problems as they arise. Non-Asians must be sensitive to cultural differences and local business styles in order to ensure a successful strategic alliance.

Selection Tactics: Key Points For Positioning

Finding sales channels and understanding options is not enough to position your company in Asia. It is equally important to have a process in place that can aid in decision-making. Since timing is critical, this process should be set up ahead of time. Some suggestions:

Obtain executive commitment from the beginning. This is critical to the business process. If the top executives don't buy into the strategy, then resources needed for implementation could be in jeopardy. It is important that risks and benefits are well understood. You don't want to get into negotiations only to find out that the will is lacking at the top.

Form a team. When evaluating the market, determining business opportunities and negotiating, it is good to pool resources and expertise. This educates those in-house and secures commitment to the program. The different perspectives of personnel in sales, marketing, manufacturing, finance and other departments can be invaluable. In fact, the team approach works best in Asia. This is because many Asian companies take a group-oriented approach to negotiation and decision-making. Your group can then negotiate with theirs. The approach also prevents one person from having to bear all the stress and responsibility of decision-making. All team members need not be at all meetings or in Asia at the same time, but they should all be knowledgeable of Asian business practices and behavior and be committed to the process.

Evaluate information carefully. Research thoroughly. Closely examine the benefits and drawbacks of each option and the effect it will have on the corporation. Remember, decisions are only as good as the information on which they are based. Bad information leads to bad decisions.

Be patient. Things take time in Asia. Scrutinize options until a good deal comes along. Be selective and look at all available alternatives. When pressed for a commitment before you are ready, learn to defuse the pressure. Stick to your game plan when appropriate but be flexible when faced with new information, circumstances, or alternatives. Nothing is absolute when structuring business in Asia.

Once agreement has been reached, prepare to implement quickly. This is where timing can be critical. Asia is a paradox in this regard because although preparation, evaluation, negotiation and decision-making may take time, once decisions are made things happen quickly, which in part explains why the business environment changes so rapidly in Asia. Consequently, market timing becomes important and getting to market quickly can be critical. Implementation needs to be thought out carefully in the planning stages and incorporated into your strategy.

5. Getting It in Writing
Legal Issues: What to Look For

When doing business in Asia, be sure to enlist good legal counsel. Developing distributor networks, forming license agreements, negotiating joint ventures, or incorporating subsidiaries can be tricky. Although there is no substitute for good luck, a good lawyer can be the next best thing!

Bear in mind that Asia is home to relationship-oriented societies. Among other things, this means that Asians tend to be less legalistic than most Western societies. For example, there are more lawyers in the city of Chicago and its outlying suburbs than in all of Japan. Lawyers are less likely to be involved in direct negotiations in the Land of the Rising Sun. Having a lawyer present at a negotiation can backfire in Asia if your counterparts feel this conveys distrust. Good legal counsel is critical, however, when finalizing contracts and otherwise sealing deals.

Although this chapter is not a legal primer, there are some legal concerns that every executive needs to be aware of when doing business in Asia. Laws governing the following areas merit special attention:

Sales channels. Determine the legal distinction between agents, representatives and distributors. Research your own country's laws regarding the use of these sales channels in foreign territories. Understand the liabilities inherent in each type of relationship.

Taxation, duties and foreign income. Can adversely affect profits or even the ability to conduct certain types of business.

Labor and employment. Especially important if you are employing your own people. Such laws may also govern the use of local agents.

Import and export. May limit your use of certain sales channels.

Territorial restrictions. Can have an impact on sales channels set up by territory. Such boundaries may not be legally enforceable, which could lead to channel conflicts.

Sales to governments. Understand local as well as home-country laws and regulations in this regard, particularly concerning restricted goods, trade sanctions, embargos, bribery and related trade issues.

Registration requirements regarding the set-up of local operations. Differ depending on whether one launches a sales office, distribution facility, joint venture or subsidiary. Also be aware of rules regarding organizational structure, disclosure of information and financing.

Intellectual property rights. Of special importance for licensing arrangements regarding the development of technology.

Many companies run into trouble in Asia when they fail to consider legal issues before entering the market. To avoid this, incorporate legal planning into your strategic planning. Of utmost importance is the protection of patents, trademarks, trade names, copyrights and trade secrets. You should give ample thought to protecting these items *before* entering Asia. It's important to assess the risks involved and what expenses may be entailed.

Consideration should be given to registering your company's name and trademark: many companies have entered Asian markets only to find their company name already registered by someone else. This can lead to painful negotiations and unexpected costs if the firm has to buy the rights to its own name. Up-front research and planning is necessary when it comes to intellectual property. This is usually a company's most valuable asset and should not be taken lightly.

Another intellectual property concern is the need for confidentiality, particularly important when working through intermediaries. Many forms of information may be considered confidential and should be covered in a confidentiality agreement. The process of doing business will likely expose agents and distributors to sensitive information regarding your business. Therefore, understanding the mutual need for confidentiality is essential.

Don't overlook local laws regarding competition. Many countries have their own anti-trust and anti-monopoly laws. In some cases, these laws are closely modeled after those in the West (this is especially true of Japan and Korea). Numerous countries have agencies that monitor corporate behavior and compliance, paying special attention to acquisitions, mergers, pricing, customer-restriction agreements, restrictions on parallel importing, and exclusivity arrangements. Your firm's home country may also have anti-trust and anti-monopoly laws that cover foreign operations. Be aware of export restrictions from your home country as well.

Laws pertaining to ethics and bribery should be carefully studied when doing business in Asia. We overlook these laws at our peril. Ethics differ from country to country; laws determining ethical behavior can be different as well. It is not enough for a businessperson to understand local business and social behavior, it is also important to know what is and is not legal in this regard. Areas to watch are payments, special accounting arrangements, and gift giving. Laws in your home country may stipulate what constitutes proper and ethical business abroad as well.

The Bribery Issue

Clients and seminar participants who do business in some Asian markets tell us that demands for bribes from government officials are a major problem. What Westerners today define as 'official corruption' prompts many business people to make under-the-table payments to get the job done. In some Asian countries these payments are sanctioned by custom even though formally illegal under local law. Regardless of how bribes are regarded locally, however, managers attending our seminars want to know how to avoid them.

Currently, the U.S. is the only country in the world whose government aggressively enforces laws against bribing officials abroad. The Foreign Corrupt Practices Act of 1977 (as amended) prescribes heavy fines and even prison sentences for any of its citizens caught bribing foreign officials. The FCPA exempts 'facilitation payments', which it does not define. It appears that small payments to expedite paperwork, for example, are not considered bribes under the law. American business people should seek competent legal advice about specific situations.

Although the situation is slowly changing, many European governments not only condone such payments, they allow their companies to claim foreign bribes as a tax deduction. Nevertheless, business people of any nationality have good reasons for avoiding the bribery trap.

First, many Western societies regard bribery as an unethical practice which corrupts both the giver and the recipient of the bribe.
Second, the regulations of many corporations strictly prohibit any
form of bribery, whether to officials or to private individuals. Third,
illegal payments tend to snowball. Bribes can quickly become a major
business expense.

Finally, even Asian countries where official corruption is wide-
spread have laws on the books prohibiting the bribing of their government employees. Though such laws may be only sporadically en-
forced, the foreigner unlucky enough to get caught is likely to face a
capricious legal system as well as very unpleasant prison conditions.

Transparency International, an organization founded by former
World Bank executives, has been publishing an annual Corruption
Perceptions Index since 1995, which ranks over 90 countries based on
international surveys by business groups and various analysts. Recently,
Bangladesh showed up as the most corrupt, with Pakistan, China, India,
and Indonesia also ranked high in terms of official corruption. However,
Singapore, another Asian country, regularly makes the Top Ten 'clean'
countries, along with New Zealand, Canada, and the Scandinavian
countries. The U.S. usually ranks below the ten cleanest nations.

Political & Economic Risk Consultancy Ltd. also regularly ranks
countries for degree of corruption and graft. In 2000, they assessed 12
Asian countries and ranked Indonesia, India, Vietnam, China, and the
Philippines in order as the most corrupt, followed by South Korea,
Thailand, Taiwan, and Malaysia. Japan and Hong Kong were found
relatively graft-free, with Singapore coming out squeaky clean.

Low government salaries combined with bureaucratic over-regula-
tion probably account for most illegal payments demanded by officials
in the so-called 'corrupt' Asian markets. Numerous vague regulations
give officials wide latitude for discretion, tempting them to demand
bribes for making a favorable decision. But international marketers
who think ahead and follow a few simple rules can avoid most demands for bribes.

- Don't assume you have to give a bribe, even in supposedly highly
  corrupt societies. Those who expect to pay a bribe will almost
  always end up doing exactly that.
- If asked for a bribe, try a polite refusal. Explain that your corporate
  policy (and Federal law, in the case of Americans) forbids such
  payments. This tactic works best for companies with sought-after

products or with a very big pencil. For example, while Sam Walton, founder of retail giant Wal-Mart, visited Indonesia in the 1980s, he told then-President Sukarno that his huge company would buy no goods 'in any market where it is necessary to bribe officials for the privilege of doing business.'

Sukarno took immediate action, ordering organizational and procedural changes which for some years thereafter sharply reduced the level of corruption. The result was that not only Wal-Mart but other big firms including Sears and J.C. Penney were able to increase their imports from Indonesia.

- Look for legal and ethical ways to get the job done. For example, offer an expense-paid visit to your company's plant, to a training course in your home country, or to attend a business-related meeting, seminar, trade show or conference in a third country. Such perks are often well received in countries where shortage of foreign exchange makes overseas travel a rare privilege. And at the same time, a legitimate business purpose is served.
- Do your homework.(See case below)

A foreign company headquartered in Singapore had to send technicians to Indonesian factories on a regular basis. About half of the company's techs had to slip a fifty dollar bill to the Jakarta airport immigration official on duty in order to get an entry visa stamped in their passports. It was always the same techs who were asked for the bribe.

Trying to figure out why only some of his travelers had to pay, the managing director one day examined his employees' travel documents. In the passports of the technicians who were paying the bribes, he noticed tiny pencil tick marks in one corner of their visa stamps. But the visa stamps of those who weren't paying showed no such marks.

The boss realized that immigration officials were routinely demanding 50 Singapore dollars from travelers new to Indonesia. They then marked the visa stamps of those who complied to show fellow officials that 'this guy pays.' On the other hand, if visitors refused the officials just shrugged and stamped the passport anyway, because of course no such payment is required. So that day the director erased all the pencil marks from his techs' passports and briefed them on the scam. After that his company's travelers paid no more bribes to Indonesian immigration officials.

Culture and Corruption

Study the culture of the country: it may show you ways to evade the bribery trap. For example, one day a U.S. manager with years of experience in Southeast Asia was rushing to catch a departing flight at Jakarta airport. A Customs and Immigration official asked to see the expensive gold pen the manager had in his shirt pocket. 'This is very nice. You don't mind if I keep it, do you?'

Although in a hurry to catch his flight, the traveler remembered the reverence most Indonesians have for their parents. 'I'd love to let you have it, Sir,' replied the manager, 'but you see, it was a gift from my late father.'

'Oh, sorry! Of course I couldn't take a gift from your father,' said the official, hastily handing back the pen.

Now, that pen was in fact not a gift. And handing a pen to the immigration officer would probably be classified as a facilitation payment, not a bribe. Nevertheless that manager didn't want to lose it, and he never again carried such a tempting writing instrument in his pocket while passing through airports in South and Southeast Asia.

The bottom line here is that business visitors should always look for ways to avoid the bribery trap in the Asia-Pacific region. If all else fails, use what you know about local customs and traditions to find a solution.

When You Need a Lawyer

One of the questions most frequently asked by people doing business in Asia is, 'When should I get the lawyers involved?' From a practical standpoint, a lawyer should be involved throughout: before the opening moves, during the negotiations, and at the end game. Legal involvement before your opening moves is necessary to understand the legal difficulties you are likely to encounter – essential to avoid pitfalls and up-front mistakes. Involvement during negotiations enables you to better assess your choices and the consequences of your decisions. When wrapping up negotiations, legal counsel can help ensure that contracts are written properly and all relevant issues are finalized.

The most prudent time to bring a lawyer into the picture depends on where you are doing business. In deal-oriented societies not having a lawyer at your side may be considered naïve. But in relationship-oriented societies having a lawyer physically present (particularly up front) may convey a sense of mistrust. In Asia, one's primary efforts should be directed toward building a good relationship. It is virtually impossible to do business in the region without this key building block. For this reason, it is prudent to use lawyers actively yet discreetly. Keep your lawyer in the background for guidance and advice. In cultures that emphasize harmony over confrontation, the presence of an attorney may cause loss of face, which can work against you.

There have been situations, however, in which the presence of lawyers has actually strengthened a business relationship. In one case, an American company trying to establish a joint venture in Korea asked their potential partner what law firm they used. The Koreans surprised the Americans by answering that they would use the same lawyers the Americans were using. The Americans didn't quite know what to do because they were used to using lawyers against opposing lawyers, which is normal in deal-oriented societies. The Koreans, on the other hand, used lawyers to certify legal boundaries and facilitate the writing of the contract. They figured that the real negotiations take place between the business parties and the lawyer would simply be there to help with any misunderstandings and write up the contract. They didn't view the lawyer for the American side as an adversary. Ultimately, the Americans agreed to use the same attorney and successfully negotiated the JV agreement.

Needless to say, using the same attorney as your counterpart has its downside, just as choosing the wrong attorney can cause great harm. Always, make sure your attorney represents your best interests. In some cases, your interests converge with those of your partner, in other cases they may not. Ascertaining your attorney's ability to handle your needs is a critical step in the negotiation process.

The Distribution Agreement: Your Cornerstone Contract

The most common contract marketers enter into in Asia is the sales and distribution agreement. The distribution agreement defines the relationship between the two parties involved and sets up legal boundaries. A general rule in Asia is to simplify agreements yet make sure critical areas are covered. Of course, this is easier said than done. The more concise the contract, however, the more easily it can be understood.

Concise contracts are also easier to translate. It is important to note that some companies in Asia expect official legal documents to be translated into their own language. This produces at least two versions of the contract, sometimes more. It is important that agreements are translated properly and convey the same meaning. The use of language and terminology is important to the understanding and resolution of disputes. Make sure the translator is well qualified.

Some key points to remember when writing up an international distribution agreement:

1. How the territory, products and/or customers are defined in the contract determine the structure of the business relationship. Be sure the role of the distributor fits into your strategy for the region. Issues such as cross-selling to other sales channels or distributors, the handling of competitive products, exclusivity, customers that are off-limits and house accounts should all be addressed in the agreement. The territory should be defined explicitly, not in vague terms. Provisions for territorial change can be included, if necessary. Note that if a distributor is to cover more than one country, separate agreements may be necessary for each country.

2. Specify the terms of sale and how orders will be handled, including purchasing procedures, delivery terms and payment and collection requirements. Don't forget tax liability issues.

3. How each side will be compensated often requires more negotiation than any other part of the agreement. Be sure to cover commission payments, promotional compensation, co-op advertising allowances, discounts (if applicable) and any other areas of potential concern.

4. Establish quotas or sales goals where necessary to help measure performance and to act as a catalyst for change or termination if required. Stocking levels and requirements, repurchase rights and warranty conditions should be clearly defined. Also, stipulate what information needs to supplied on a regular basis; for example, sales reports or market data. Remember, the distributor is not your customer but your vehicle to market. Acquiring information on end-user customers can be critical to your sales and marketing efforts.

5. Define issues regarding business conduct. This includes adherence to all local as well as foreign laws that affect your business within the territory. It also includes confidentiality and the protection of intellectual property such as brand name and trademark rights. This is of particular importance as a sales agent or distributor will

want to use these for promotion and sales. Make sure your company retains these rights.

6. Explain how notices are handled. This can be very important, especially those regarding payment, delays in delivery and termination.

7. Often overlooked are issues of ownership. Provisions should be considered in case of a change in ownership. You may also want to include a clause or two requiring your business partners to disclose cross-ownership relationships with other businesses, especially distributors that carry or develop competing lines. It is not unusual in Asia for owners of distributorships to have stakes in other firms, including other distributorships which sell competing products.

8. Stipulate which laws and which jurisdiction govern the contract. This is important for interpretation and dispute resolution. It is preferable, of course, to have your home country's laws apply, but this may not be possible. In some countries the local civil and commercial codes automatically govern any contracts signed by a local business entity. Also, determine which language governs the contract in case of a dispute.

Two of the most important parts of an international sales or distribution agreement are the duration of the agreement and the termination procedures. Make sure these issues are clearly addressed in the negotiations. This can be difficult in Asia as the main reason for making an agreement is to build a lasting relationship, not to end one. Yet the issues need to be dealt with and dealt with carefully. Without a termination clause, a company can be at the mercy of local laws governing the definition and dissolution of such agreements.

In some cases, a company may be liable to the distributor if there is no just cause or sufficient notice given, resulting in compensation payments for indemnity or damages. Not only can this be a financial burden, it can damage your company's creditability and hinder, change, or delay the implementation of a repositioning program. For these reasons, a termination clause needs to be carefully considered and reviewed from a legal standpoint.

Some tips:

Consider establishing a fixed termination date. This limits the term of the agreement and makes clear that it is not indefinite. However, this clause requires the two parties to renegotiate the basic agreement on a periodic basis.

In lieu of a fixed termination date, set an initial term with a clause for automatic renewal if everything goes right. Bear in mind, however, that in some cases automatic renewal may be construed as grounds for an indefinite relationship, so your legal counsel should review this clause country by country.

Specify grounds for termination. This can include not meeting sales goals or quotas, change of ownership, illegal or unethical behavior, insolvency or not rectifying a breach of contract. Usually a period of notice is required, which might be specified by local law.

Include a calculation for compensation in the event of termination. This shows good faith and may be used to avoid subsequent compensation claims. Alternatively, insert a clause that waives the right to compensation altogether.

Consider including a provision for dispute resolution in the agreement. Obviously, negotiation should be the first course of action for resolving problems. This can be done either directly or through an intermediary. In Asia, using an intermediary can facilitate communication and prevent loss of face. Generally, disputes in relationship-oriented cultures are resolved through negotiation, a process that will result in some form of compromise. However, should negotiations prove intractable, it will be necessary to fall back on your agreement. Therefore, a dispute-resolution clause should be included.

Two ways to resolve disputes are by law or arbitration. As mentioned above, you will usually prefer your home country laws to apply, but your business counterpart may not agree to this. This can become a flashpoint in your negotiations. If you do not want the laws of your Asian partner's to apply, compromise by agreeing on those of a third country.

Dispute resolution through arbitration is another alternative. If you prefer this method, insert a clause in the contract calling for binding arbitration. Check local laws to make sure arbitral decisions are enforceable; in most countries they are. In the United States, for example, such rulings have been accepted by the Supreme Court.

Arbitral services and institutions are available worldwide. Be sure to stipulate which rules apply, however. The United Nations Convention on the International Sale of Goods can be useful in this regard. Also note that although arbitration can often be an effective dispute-resolution mechanism, in certain cases – such as the protection of intellectual property rights – it may be better to stipulate that disputes should be adjudicated by a court of law located in the designated jurisdiction.

Contract Negotiations: Dealing with the Asian Perspective

Some rules to remember when negotiating a contract in Asia:

The initial contact is important, as it sets the tone for the negotiation. Take special care with how you make the first contact and how introductions are initiated.

Relationship building always comes before deal making. A good personal relationship with your counterpart is essential for solving the problems that will inevitably arise.

Preparation is important. Know what you want to accomplish. Be prepared for counter proposals. Consider all available alternatives when you encounter roadblocks. Keep your options open.

Understand local business practices. Be knowledgeable and prepare to adapt. This does not mean you should compromise your goals. Often there are different ways to achieve the same result.

Be patient. The length of time necessary to court a business partner depends on the country and culture. In general, much more time is required in Asia than in Western cultures. One reason is that building a personal relationship is essential and this cannot be done overnight. Also, in countries like Japan, business decisions are usually made by consensus, a time-consuming process. Elsewhere in Asia, most decisions are made by the CEO, which means little gets done if the boss is busy or unavailable. In bureaucratic environments, executives tend to postpone decision-making, especially if risk is involved. In general, more face-to-face bargaining is required in Asia than in other parts of the world, so many meetings may be necessary before you can strike a deal.

Control your emotions. When negotiating, avoid losing your temper. Try not to show emotion – except when making a concession. Then do let your face show the pain!

Learn to decipher nonverbal signals. In Asia, negotiators tend to communicate more with body language than with words. It is also important to listen. Concentrate on what is meant, which is not necessarily what is said.

Avoid causing your Asian counterpart to lose face. This is the quickest way to delay or even break a deal. It can also affect implementation and on-going business relationships even after the deal is completed. Remember, your relationship is more important than the contract.

Watch out for common tactics used in Asia to gain information or concessions. It is very common that just when you think agreement has been reached, your counterparts will come up with 'one last' demand. And then another. And then another. Be prepared and leave enough room in your offer to counter these tactics. In the PRC, the Chinese may say you are a 'friend of China' when they want another concession. Counter by smiling and moving on to the next item on the agenda. In Japan, negotiators often try to control the process by asking a lot of questions. Respond patiently and ask them questions to regain control. In India, 'we are such a poor country, please help us' is a common tactic. Counter with a smile and a reminder that you run a business, not an aid organization. Find reliable legal counsel.

As you should have legal counsel when working on contracts in particular, so should you have legal counsel when negotiating in general. Choose your legal representation carefully. When negotiating in Asia, however, it is better to use your personal relationship to solve problems rather than to rely on lawyers.

Be prepared to deal with graft and corruption. When negotiating with government officials in some Asian countries you can expect direct or indirect requests for bribes. Remember that bribing government officials may be illegal not only under home-country laws – such as the U.S. Foreign Corrupt Practices Act – but also according to local laws in the various Asian countries.

Don't forget to educate home-office personnel on proper negotiating techniques – especially those that will be in contact with your Asian counterparts. All relevant personnel must be committed to the long-term success of the business relationship.

6. Putting It All Together
Structuring Your Operations

Structuring business operations properly in Asia is as important to success as choosing the right market-entry and sales vehicles. You can structure operations in a number of ways, although it is usually done geographically, by function or by culture. One way is to divide Asia into manageable territories such as by country or region. For companies that are growing, further sub-division may be necessary later in order to maintain control over sales networks and resources. At some point operations may grow to such an extent or reach such a level of complexity that it may make more sense to structure them by function.

Functional structures are normally designed to handle more than just sales and marketing – they add value as well. Value can be added in the form of manufacturing, research and development, engineering, technical support, logistics, after-sales service, procurement or financing. Often, different functions are performed in different countries, with those units supporting the company as a whole. For example, a firm could do its research and development in Japan, manufacture its products in China, but sell worldwide. Functional structures in Asia range from simple to complex, depending on market and resource needs.

Sometimes it is necessary to organize your sales operations in Asia by culture. For example, you may want to handle all Japanese customers including Japanese transplants throughout Asia as a 'territory' and perhaps utilize common sales channels if they are available. You may want to handle certain markets that are culturally similar as one, for example a Greater China territory that covers Taiwan, Hong Kong, and the People's Republic of China but of course be sensitive to political differences.

Many businesses in Asia are based on traditional relationships and alliances. In some cases, it may be necessary to find 'connected' sales channels that allow you access to these alliances. This is especially true of Asian business networks such as Japanese *keiretsu*, Korean *chaebol* and, to a lesser extent, large Asian firms run by ethnic Chinese.

A *keiretsu* is a group of companies that is held together by long-standing business relationships and sometimes cross-shareholding agreements. Some groups are large enough to include banking, insurance, manufacturing, transportation, real estate development, retailing, power, chemical, construction, food-processing and trading concerns. *Keiretsu* trace their origin to pre-World War II holding companies known as *zaibatsu* – conglomerates based on historical family alliances. Some examples of famous modern *keiretsu* include Mitsubishi, Sanwa, Sumitomo, Daiichi-Kangyo, and Mitsui.

South Korean *chaebol* are also alliances of different types of businesses. Some have their roots in family and historical relationships but many were encouraged and financed by the government to spur industrialization. As a result, *chaebol* tend to enjoy close ties to the government. Some famous *chaebol* include Lucky Goldstar, Hyundai, Daewoo, Samsung, and Sungyong. *Chaebol* are more hierarchical than *keiretsu,* more centrally controlled and often still family-owned and controlled.

Another type of Asian business network is that owned and run by ethnic Chinese. Many of these are based in Southeast Asia, like the Thailand-based Charoen Pokphand Group. Ethnic-Chinese conglomerates are usually a collection of strategic alliances formed as a result of family ties and *guanxi.* They tend to be more informally structured than *keiretsu* or *chaebol,* and more entrepreneurial. Because ethnic Chinese have settled throughout Asia, these conglomerates can be far reaching.

Littelfuse is an example of an American company successfully plugged into some of these business networks. This U.S.-based firm, an electronics-component manufacturer, focuses on supplying fuses to two major markets in Asia: general electronics, which includes computers, appliances and telecom equipment; and automotive. When Littelfuse first began selling in Asia, it had limited resources and chose to enter the market by exporting to distributors located in different countries. It was a simple geographic structure.

For the automotive sector, Littelfuse chose to license production and marketing to a Japanese manufacturer because the automotive market is specialized, investment-intensive, and requires good personal contacts in Asia. This manufacturer is part of a *keiretsu* that is a key player in Japan's automotive industry.

With regard to general electronics, Littelfuse's Asian business grew in part because it had a local presence, but also because of the global shift of manufacturing to the region. Soon the company found it necessary to set up a direct facility, a warehouse, and sales operation in Singapore. This operation helped manage and service its Asian distributor network, which handled the entire region except for Japanese customers. Littelfuse utilized a special distributor not only handle to customers in Japan but also Japanese 'transplants' throughout Asia. Thus, the company had two separate distribution networks: one based on geography for non-Japanese customers and another based on common culture for its Japanese customers.

As Littelfuse's business continued to grow in Asia, it saw the need to set up a greater direct presence. After Singapore and Japan, the next market it wanted to get directly involved in was South Korea. Its first step was to form a joint venture with a local manufacturer. Later, Littelfuse was able to buy up one of its prime local competitors. The existing joint venture was merged with the newly purchased company and the new entity became a Littelfuse subsidiary – a subsidiary with access to major *chaebols* in the Korean electronic and automotive sectors.

To satisfy growing Asian demand and, at the same time, reduce costs, the company further expanded its presence in the region with the creation of other manufacturing subsidiaries. A facility was purchased in the Philippines, another was set up in China. Both countries are low-cost manufacturing bases, but the China operation brought the added benefit of supplying a locally-made product to the fast-growing PRC market.

Littelfuse further bolstered its Asian network by adding a sales office in Hong Kong, which manages regional sales and provides additional support for its China operations.

By this time Asia had become more than just a manufacturing base and a market for Littelfuse's goods. Customers were developing new products in the region and for the U.S. company to grow it had to be part of this effort. Littelfuse therefore established a technical support facility in Japan to provide regional engineering assistance to other Littelfuse facilities and to tap into customer R&D efforts for new product opportunities. This subsidiary was later expanded to handle sales, distribution and specialized assembly for the Japanese.

Managing Your Operations

Most companies start out managing their Asian network from home-country headquarters; particularly when business is first starting to develop and when sales channels are relatively straightforward and uncomplicated. As local operations are added in Asia, management from headquarters can be beneficial in helping evaluate business requirements and aiding overall decision-making. To effectively manage from the home office one must have an understanding of and sensitivity to foreign cultures and the commitment to proactively maintain communications across time zones. Because this requires special expertise, some companies hire Asian specialists for this purpose. They may also structure their export operations to provide special service for the Asia market.

The Asia regional manager should do more than just oversee and manage local activity. He/she should also identify new business opportunities and trends. This may require frequent travel to the region by key staff. There is no substitute for face-to-face contact when conducting business in Asia.

When it becomes necessary to expand and create local operations in Asia, management becomes more complicated because you may have to restructure your staff both in the target markets and at the home office. Many firms opt to establish a regional headquarters at this point. Such a move demonstrates commitment to the region, but the decision should be made with care. Two issues that need to be handled delicately are where to base your regional headquarters and who will report to it. Should one country seem to be favored with the location for regional headquarters, this may cause a loss of face to managers in other countries. If country managers previously reported to home-office headquarters and are suddenly asked to report to a regional office, this may likewise be viewed negatively.

A classic problem faced by managers is how much autonomy to grant a local operation. Too much control stifles creativity, the sense of ownership, and productivity. Not enough control fosters disassociation, conflicting interests and can likewise affect productivity. There is no simple solution to this dilemma. The degree of control ultimately depends on two factors: the philosophy of the corporation and the attitudes and expertise of the managers themselves.

Role of the International Manager

The success or failure of your operations in Asia ultimately depends on people: the people who research, formulate, and execute the business plan, and the managers who craft the human relationships upon which doing business depends. The more these people understand human behavior, the higher chance they have of achieving their goals. Here are some characteristics and skills a manager must have in order to succeed in Asia:

Adaptability. Able to adjust to new information and circumstances quickly.

Relationship-building skills. Ability to nurture trust and confidence in those one works with. It is important that this is done in a non-controlling way. Managers who are overly controlling usually falter over time in Asia.

Communication Skills. It is essential to make yourself understood. It is not essential to be able to speak an Asian language (although this certainly helps), but one needs to express oneself in a way that communicates trust and understanding. Frequent communication, including repeated face-to-face contact, is important. Exchanging information is beneficial since Asians tend to value shared knowledge.

Sensitivity. Besides knowing Asian business protocol, this entails the ability to interpret body language, appearance, posture, expressions, eye movement, variations of speech, gestures, touch and non-touch signals as well as interpersonal distance.

Networking Skills. The most effective networking is done informally. The Asian manager often becomes the intermediary between a local operation and headquarters – a key role for Asians, especially during times of conflict, as go-betweens are valued for their interpretive skills and face-saving abilities.

Planning Skills. This includes the ability to both strategize and organize to achieve results. The key is to think ahead, be proactive and focus on a long-term goal so that minor problems are put in perspective.

Longevity. In the United States it is common for executives to change jobs and move around frequently. In Asia, however, it is difficult enough to build relationships without introducing new faces into the equation. Staying on the job for a long time can benefit relationship-development and management. It also gives managers a chance to learn and grow. They need time to obtain knowledge and gain respect.

Negotiating Skills. The manager responsible for Asian markets is an on-going negotiator. Developing business and building channels is a never-ending process. The manager must represent both the interests of headquarters and those of his or her Asian counterparts. It is important that Asian employers view themselves as partners with valued knowledge and capabilities.

Another point to consider when managing Asian operations is group identification. It is imperative for a manager to identify with the organizations he or she manages. This helps develop cohesiveness and foster loyalty. Keep in mind, though, that if the manager is an expatriate, it is not necessary to 'go native.' He or she doesn't have to become part of the clan, so to speak. Trying too hard to be accepted can undermine authority, recognition and effectiveness, and may even bring about resentment. One needs to maintain the independence and identity of an outsider while recognizing the values, behavior and norms of the groups one is managing.

This also holds true for Asians assigned to jobs in the region. Some executives believe it is easier to hire a local person to manage local business affairs. Sometimes this is true, but not always. In one such case, a company hired a competent person who was born and reared in Korea but went to college and lived for a time in the United States. He spoke Korean and English fluently, but when he was sent back in Korea to work, he found he was never fully accepted as a local. He was perceived as an outsider and treated as one.

Regardless of the ethnicity of the Asian manager, he or she should also be able to convey respect and neutralize confrontation – focus on harmony, not conflict. The ability to preserve harmony and save face are highly esteemed personal as well as managerial traits. Since the concept of face influences every aspect of relationships in most Asian societies, it affects individual as well as group performance. A good manager develops techniques for saving and giving face while not sacrificing authority. This is not to say that confrontation or conflict should always be avoided. Sometimes they may be necessary. However, where possible, confrontations should be brief, focused, and carefully controlled with an emphasis on desired results and avoidance of embarrassment.

Another key consideration for management in Asia is the concept of status. In Asia, status and authority can be conveyed by a person's nationality, education, experience, gender, or age. These factors should be considered when selecting managers. It is important that Asian counterparts know the manager's position, title and credentials, which should be listed on the manager's business card.

7. What about Bill?

So what about Bill Stafford and MIB? Well, by the time Bill got back to the office he had composed himself. He realized he could not change what was happening, so he set about dealing with the situation.

The first thing Bill did was to assemble his staff and explain the situation. After considerable discussion, the group decided to devise a plan. Because what was involved was more complex than anything MIB had encountered in the past, they decided to bring in an outside consultant. The consultant happened to be experienced at doing business in China, so he coached MIB staff on Chinese culture and negotiating techniques.

Bill then decided to see China first-hand. He and an MIB staff member flew to Shanghai and met with several China-based Western executives in order to learn about their experiences. They also took in some sight seeing. On the way, Bill stopped in Japan to meet face-to-face in order to build a relationship with a trading company that had inquired about his products.

Upon his return, Bill assembled a team of staff members from manufacturing, sales and finance to decide how MIB would position itself in Asia.

Early in the planning process, MIB considered whether to go it alone or find a local partner. Management ruled out exporting because they did not feel this was the most effective way to deal with local competitors. Instead, they decided to plunge in right away, leveraging their resources and know-how to gain a strategic advantage over these potential rivals.

Management also decided that marketing their core product was enough, as this was a component going into the same customer assemblies in Asia as it was in the United States. MIB could duplicate or transfer existing tooling. Staffing would be critical because the Asian operation would need local maintenance and know-how, but the executives realized that finding capable local personnel would be a problem.

Because of the complexity of issues such as government regulations, setting up a manufacturing facility, logistics, parts importation, distribution, staffing, customer service concerns and cultural considerations, MIB decided that finding a local partner would be the best way to go in China.

Bill's staff used industry connections as well as U.S. and Chinese government trade organizations to help establish contacts. They asked the Japanese trading company Bill had met with in Tokyo for suggestions. Bill now realized that he had a potential market in Japan, making it even more worthwhile to have a low-cost manufacturing facility in China.

After doing preparatory research, Bill and his staff took another trip to China, this time to meet with potential partners and study the costs of supporting customers. The trip was long and demanding. They traveled great distances and visited many different cities using all types of transportation, staying at many different hotels and enduring long nights of entertaining.

Based on information gathered during the trip, Bill and his staff learned the advantages and disadvantages of various market-entry strategies as well as the strengths and weaknesses of potential partners. He decided MIB had two options. They could either set up a licensed manufacturing arrangement with a local partner and have the products sold exclusively through an MIB sales organization, or establish a joint venture with a local partner who would both manufacture and sell the products in China.

As of today, this is where things stand. MIB will further evaluate the benefits and drawbacks of these two options. More market visits are planned and negotiations will continue. Bill sees good prospects for MIB and is pleased with how his staff is handling the project. In fact, Bill is now considering setting up a small engineering office in Japan to focus on opportunities in that country.

PART TWO

Negotiating in Asia

8. East Asia

Japanese Negotiating Behavior

Over the past decade, the business culture of Japan has changed in ways that are important for international marketers and investors. The demand for imported consumer goods has risen sharply, and discount retailers have expanded at the expense of high-end department stores. Japanese manufacturers have increasingly moved production offshore, contributing to the marked rise in unemployment and an erosion in the 'job-for-life' tradition. Meanwhile we've seen the rise of freelancing, temp agencies and headhunting firms.

In addition, there has been a large number of product recalls in a country renowned for high quality. For example, Japan-watchers were shocked in early 2001 when Matsushita announced its second mobile phone recall while Sony announced its fourth. Few observers anticipated the rapid move of the country's famous trading companies into sophisticated outsourcing functions, IT, e-commerce and bio-technology. Alert marketers will want to determine which of these recent changes and trends create new opportunities and which present new competitive challenges.

The Japanese negotiating style, in contrast, has changed little in recent years. It's still true that on any given day you may face counterparts who have lived and worked in Munich, London, Sydney or Los Angeles – people who are easily able to close the culture gap with visiting Western dealmakers. But the very next day you may face more traditional negotiating partners, and it will be mostly up to you to overcome the substantial cultural barriers in order to reach agreement.

Knowing how to bridge the culture gap is especially critical for firms trying to market in Japan, because there the buyer enjoys much higher status than the seller. And the seller is expected to adapt to the buyer. But how to adapt if we don't understand the local business customs and practices? For starters, it helps to remember that most Japanese are relationship-focused, formal, hierarchical and reserved. Now let's look at local negotiating behavior in detail.

Make Initial Contact Indirectly. Most Japanese companies do not do business with strangers. A good way to make contact is at a trade show or on an official trade mission. You may also arrange for an introduction by a respected third party of high status, ideally someone known to both you and your Japanese counterpart. If you do not have a prestigious mutual friend, ask your bank, chamber of commerce, law firm, your embassy or JETRO to introduce you.

Build a Relationship Before Talking Business. In Japan, developing rapport is an important and time-consuming component of the overall negotiating process. Get to know your counterparts before starting to discuss business. Socializing over drinks, meals, karaoke and golf are proven ways to build rapport.

Language. Because of the educational system, relatively few Japanese business people speak and understand English well enough to feel comfortable negotiating in the language. So interpreters play an important role, and visitors have to decide whether to hire their own or rely on their counterparts for translation.

Orientation to Time. Japanese value punctuality and strict adherence to schedules. And they expect the same of their foreign counterparts -- especially potential suppliers!

Hierarchy, Status, and Respect. Younger, subordinate individuals are expected to defer to older, higher-ranking persons. Since few women have reached positions of authority in this traditional, hierarchical society, most men are not used to dealing with females on the basis of equality in a business context.

Less well-known is that fact that in Japan the buyer automatically enjoys higher status than the seller in a commerical transaction. To reflect that status difference, buyers expect to be treated with deference. Hence young foreigners – especially women – face significant cultural obstacles when trying to sell to Japanese customers.

Here are four ways to overcome age and gender barriers with the Japanese:

1. Get introduced by the eldest, most senior male colleague available.

2. Learn how to show proper respect. By showing respect you earn respect.
3. Establish your professional or technical credentials, taking care not to appear cocky or boastful. Expertise confers status.
4. Many women are more skilled than males in reading body language. This ability is particularly valuable when dealing with Japanese, who rely heavily on nonverbal communication.

Maintaining Surface Harmony. Japanese regard open displays of anger or impatience as infantile and offensive. They lose respect for people who cannot retain a calm exterior under stress. Visiting negotiators are advised to avoid open confrontation at all cost.

Face Issues. 'Face' has to do with self-respect, dignity, reputation. You can *lose face* by appearing childish or lacking in self-control – for example by losing your temper. You can cause your counterparts to lose face by expressing sharp disagreement, embarrassing them, criticizing them in public or by showing disrespect in other ways. Causing loss of face can completely disrupt a promising business negotiation.

You can *give* your counterpart face by using polite forms of address and observing local customs and traditions. Giving face is an effective way to build a solid relationship. If you make a mistake you may be able to *save your face* with a humble apology. And you can save the other party's face for example by allowing him a graceful exit from a difficult negotiating position.

Formality and Rituals. To help maintain surface harmony and prevent loss of face, Japanese rely on ritualized codes of behavior. An example is the formalized exchange of business cards, the ritual of the *meishi* (see under Business Protocol below). Japanese negotiators tend to dress and behave rather formally and are more comfortable with visitors who do likewise.

Communication Style. Reserved and formal while they are getting to know you. Less reliance on written and telephone communication, more emphasis on face-to-face meetings.

Indirect Verbal Communication. Japanese negotiators frequently employ indirect, vague, oblique language wherein the meaning is deliberately ambiguous and implicit rather than clear and explicit.

They tend to employ circumlocutions, understatement, silence and evasive language to avoid offending the other party.

For instance, many Japanese consider it offensive to reply to a request with a blunt 'no'. So a negotiator might answer 'We will do our best,' or 'That will be difficult' instead. The result of this politeness might be confusion on the part of the foreigner, but surface harmony has been maintained at the cost of clarity.

Japanese distrust glibness. They use fewer words than people from more expressive cultures, relying more on paraverbal and nonverbal language.

Paraverbal Communication. Japanese tend to speak softly and hesitantly and employ frequent silences. They may pause at considerable length before answering a question or responding to a request, and they avoid interrupting others, which would be very rude. A laugh or giggle may signal nervousness or embarrassment rather than amusement. Visitors should avoid loud talking and always wait until their Japanese counterpart has finished speaking before saying their piece.

Nonverbal Communication. When meeting and greeting, expect a soft handshake. Avoid strong, direct eye contact, which may be misinterpreted as an attempt to intimidate or an indication of hostility. A smile may mask disapproval or anger.

Body language is restrained and formal, with small gestures. Avoid arm-waving and other vigorous gestures. Japan is a low-contact culture, so expect very little touching. Avoid arm-grabbing and backslapping.

It is rude to raise your voice or interrupt a Japanese person in midsentence. Maintain an arm's length distance and avoid physical contact other than the handshake.

Strong eye contact makes many Japanese uncomfortable. Direct your gaze at his forehead, chin or tie knot most of the time.

Gesturing vigorously, winking or shrugging your shoulders may confuse your counterparts. Avoid pointing with your index finger. Instead, indicate direction with a sweeping motion of your whole hand, palm up.

Negotiating Style

Making a Presentation. Avoid opening with a joke or humorous anecdote. This would show lack of respect for the topic and for the audience. Speak clearly and simply. Avoid using double negatives and convoluted sentences, jargon, slang or unusual words. Take care not to over-praise your product or company. Instead employ testimonials or articles written about your firm. Use visual aids, especially for numbers, and provide copies of the presentation.

Bargaining Range. Starting off with a high price so as to leave room for bargaining works in many markets, but this approach may backfire with the Japanese. Always have a cogent reason for any major concession on price or terms.

Concession Behavior. Japanese often find it difficult to grant concessions during a negotiation because their bargaining position was usually arrived at via a long, drawn-out discussion process within their company. Any change in this 'package' may require lengthy internal discussions. So bring plenty of patience to the table. And save any major concession until the end game.

Decision-Making. Many Japanese companies still make decisions by consensus, a time-consuming process and one more reason to bring patience to the negotiating table. Japanese like the people who can make decisions to be present when the decisions need to be made. Senior Japanese are not normally present during the early stages of negotiations unless a counterpart of the same rank is involved.

Role of the Contract. The final written agreement is less important than the strength of the relationship with your counterpart, but do put everything in writing anyway. The Japanese side may expect to renegotiate the contract if circumstances change. For them, the contract is an expression of intent.

Some Westerners like to hand the other side a draft contract to be used as the outline for the negotiation and then discuss each item point by point. With the Japanese it is better to keep the draft to yourself. Look for areas of agreement before discussing the difficult items, and call in the lawyers only towards the end of the process.

Maintaining the Relationship. It is important to stay in close contact with your Japanese customers and partners between visits, whether by telephone, fax, letter or email.

Business Protocol and Etiquette

The Initial Meeting. Will probably take place late in the afternoon at your Japanese counterpart's office. The introducer ('shokai-sha') is likely to be present. You will exchange cards, engage in general conversation but no business talk. About 6 pm your counterparts will suggest dinner; they will pay. Small gifts may be exchanged before leaving the office. After dinner, drinks at night clubs until about 11:30 pm.

Dress Code. A dark suit with white shirt and conservative tie is appropriate attire for men. Women wear conservative dresses or suits.

The Name Game. Address your counterparts by their surname plus -*san*, but do not add this suffix to your own name when introducing yourself. On Japanese-language business cards the surname is printed first, but on cards printed in English the order may be reversed. When in doubt, ask.

Counterparts with non-Japanese first names (e.g. 'Frank') may be comfortable with first names after work, but stick to surnames at meetings. If your family name is difficult, they may append the suffix 'san' to your first name, e.g. 'Richard-san.'

Exchanging Business Cards. Have cards printed in Japanese characters on one side. Offer your card, Japanese-language side uppermost, with both hands and a slight bow. Accept your counterpart's card with both hands, take a few seconds to read it. At the end of the meeting, put the card carefully away in your card wallet.

Meeting Behavior. Expect your counterparts to engage in frequent side conversations in Japanese. Participants may frequently leave and re-enter the meeting. Senior Japanese may doze off – or appear to – during meetings.

Gift Giving. Gifts should be carefully wrapped (no bows) in 'business' colors: gray, brown, blue or green. Avoid red, pink and floral patterns as well as white and black paper. Present gifts with both hands and a slight bow. Never praise your own gift. Japanese will probably set your gift aside and open it after you leave.

Good gift choices are items not made in Japan or elsewhere in Asia: premium cognacs or single-malt whiskeys (boxed), photo books, luxury foods and things your country is famous for. The best gifts reflect your knowledge of the recipient's personal interests and hobbies.

It is OK to give different gifts to different individuals according to their rank in the corporate hierarchy. Always keep a careful record of which gifts were given to which individuals.

Wining and Dining. When asked what you would like, a good response is 'Whatever you are having.' Many Japanese relax by consuming a lot of alcohol. If you do not drink, to avoid spoiling the party cite a medical reason for abstinence. Avoid pouring your own drinks. Take a sip whenever your neighbor fills your glass. When you have had enough, leave your glass half full.

Do not leave chopsticks crossed or standing in your rice bowl. Soup and tea are often noisily slurped. Use both hands when passing or receiving a bowl or dish. It is OK to lift the soup or rice bowl to your mouth. Avoid blowing your nose at a meeting, a bar or the dinner table. Instead, leave the room. On the other hand, it is quite acceptable to sniffle constantly throughout a meal.

You have to remove your shoes at many restaurants, so make sure there are no holes in your socks. Note that smoking is still common in restaurants and other places. Males visitors may be invited to a hostess bar after dinner.

Be sure to reciprocate a dinner invitation when in Japan. Often a good choice is a French or Italian restaurant. When hosting, leave the table to pay the check or make payment arrangements in advance.

Korean Negotiating Behavior

South Korea's business culture is unique within East Asia. Although similar to that of neighboring China and Japan in some respects, Korean negotiating behavior differs in important ways. Koreans tend to be more direct, more expressive and more assertive than Chinese and (especially) Japanese negotiators, for example.

The typical Korean *chaebol* also differs from the Japanese *keiretsu* in that more of them are family-owned and -managed, and they do not practice permanent employment.

Making Contact. Unless you can meet potential business partners at a trade show or on an official trade mission, the best way is to arrange a formal introduction. Contacting a person you don't know directly rarely works. The best introducer is a respected person or organization of high status, ideally someone known to both you and your Korean counterpart. Failing that, look for someone known to the company or person you wish to meet and ask him or her to introduce you. Having the right connections is absolutely vital in Korea.

Building Rapport. Developing good rapport is a key part of the negotiating process in Korea. Getting to know your counterparts before starting to discuss business lays the groundwork for successful discussions. To help create and maintain an atmosphere of smooth interpersonal relations you should socialize with your counterparts over drinks, meals and other entertainment. Golf, another good way to build relationships, is becoming more and more popular.

Communicating with Koreans. Visiting negotiators should be aware of their Korean business partners' sensitivity to harmony, mood and atmosphere. Take care to avoid spoiling their 'state of good feelings' or *kibun,* without which you won't make much progress toward agreement.

If your counterparts surprise you with an emotional outburst, stay calm and try to maintain surface harmony. Disturbing a Korean's kibun is likely to sour his mood and make things more difficult. Staying cool rather than displaying irritation or anger is the best way to get things done.

Be alert to hints and information communicated subtly via *i-sum jun-sim*. Translated roughly as 'telepathy,' this form of nonverbal language is regarded by Koreans as the highest form of interpersonal communication. Practice active listening and watch your Korean partners' faces for signs of agreement or perhaps impatience or irritation.

Verbal Language. An increasing number of South Korean managers speak fluent English these days, but it's still a good idea to ask whether an interpreter will be needed. If you conclude that an interpreter is needed, consider hiring your own rather than relying on one supplied by the other party, especially for a major negotiation.

Koreans speak less directly than northern Europeans and North Americans but are more direct than Japanese. To reduce the chance of giving offense, Koreans often resort to evasive language. Most of the time they are skilled at controlling emotion and hiding their true feelings. Although Koreans take pride in being regarded as more direct and assertive than the Japanese, they normally avoid giving a blunt 'no' to avoid giving offence. Here again, surface harmony takes precedence over clarity of the message.

Paraverbal and Nonverbal Communication. Koreans rely on a sort of sixth sense to gauge the mood and reactions of their counterpart. This sense involves reading subtle paraverbal and nonverbal signals.

- Koreans are more comfortable with silence than visitors from expressive cultures. Expect significant pauses during meetings. Korean negotiators try to avoid interrupting the other party, since this would be considered rude. Visiting negotiators should likewise wait until their Korean counterpart has finished speaking before saying their piece.
- You normally use your right hand only when passing something to a Korean. But to show special respect, use the right hand with the left hand supporting your right elbow.
- Expect moderate eye contact. Most Koreans look into your eyes about half the time during a conversation. Avoid using a very direct, intense gaze, which signals anger or hostility.

- A smile may mask disapproval or anger. Body language is re-strained, formal, with very few gestures. Avoid arm-waving and other large, vigorous gestures. Expect little touching: Korea is generally a low-contact culture when interacting with foreigners.
- Interpersonal distance varies. On the street Koreans jostle one another regularly, even when there seems to be plenty of space. In a business context however, expect to maintain about an arm's-length distance from others.

Hierarchy, Status, and Gender. Korean society is a steeply vertical one, with a strict hierarchy. Remember to show proper respect to people of high status, including older and high-ranking executives. Younger, subordinate individuals are expected to defer to older, higher-ranking persons.

Related to the importance of hierarchies, Koreans' sense of group harmony includes the concept of *inhwa*, which incorporates loyalty on the part of employees as well as the paternalistic concern of employers towards their workers.

Since very few women have reached positions of authority in local companies, many Korean men are still unaccustomed to dealing with females on the basis of equality in a business context. Women face significant cultural obstacles when trying to do business with Koreans, but this is changing. At a recent conference in the U.S., we met grad-uates of an established South Korean M.B.A. program for women. As more local women are seen in management positions, foreign women will have an easier time being accepted.

Overcoming Age and Gender Barriers. Younger negotiators, especially women from less male-dominated business cultures, may want to prepare themselves in order to avoid problems at the bargain-ing table:

- Be introduced at the meeting (or before, in person or by telephone) by the oldest, most senior male executive available. Status is to a certain extent a transferable asset.
- Following a proper introduction as outlined above, present your business card clearly, showing your title, function, advanced de-grees and professional credentials. During the preliminary conver-sation find occasion to refer to your rank, title, experience and qualifications. This should of course be done without any hint of

arrogance or boastfulness. Credentials and expertise definitely confer respect in Korea.
- Any colleague or associate accompanying you should likewise make reference to your position, if you are the one in charge. If your subordinate is addressed by Korean counterparts, you should be the one to reply. To signal your seniority nonverbally, your subordinate should turn to you and wait for you to speak.
- Learn the verbal, paraverbal, and nonverbal ways of showing proper respect to your senior Korean counterparts. Respectful behavior on your part makes it easier for them to treat you with proper respect.
- Pay special attention to the paraverbal and nonverbal signals coming from the other side of the bargaining table. Women around the world tend to be more skilled than males in reading body language. Take advantage of this ability: it can be very useful with Koreans, who engage in a great deal of nonverbal communication. Korean negotiators respect foreigners who take the time and effort to correctly interpret their body language.

Business Negotiating Style

Making a Presentation. Opening with a joke or humorous anecdote would show lack of respect for the topic and for the audience. Speak clearly and simply. Use visual aids as much as possible, especially where numbers are involved.

Concern with Face. Face is related to self-respect, dignity, reputation. Causing loss of face, even unintentionally, can destroy harmony and disrupt a promising business negotiation. It helps to use the proper forms of address and to observe local customs and traditions in Korea.

Orientation to Time. The larger, more international Korean companies value punctuality and adherence to schedules. Because of traffic congestion, however, your local counterparts might arrive for a meeting half an hour or so late. To show irritation over such an unavoidable delay would be rude. Smaller firms in the provinces may take a slightly more relaxed approach to punctuality.

Bargaining Range. Koreans are known as tough negotiators. When calculating your initial offer, allow some room for bargaining. That way you can give in gracefully when pressed for a concession – while of course demanding an equivalent concession in return.

Decision Making. Bring a large supply of patience with you to the bargaining table. Big decisions are generally made at the top of Korean companies, and chief executives are busy people.

Role of the Contract. To Koreans, the final contract is less important then the strength of the relationship between the two parties. The legal agreement is akin to an expression of intent. Hence your local counterparts may well try to renegotiate if circumstances should change. Just remember, the renegotiation of terms can work both ways.

Business Protocol and Etiquette

Dress Code. Dark suit, white shirt, conservative tie for men, conservative dress or suit for women.

Meeting and Greeting. In Korea, introductions are not made casually. Arrange for a formal introduction to your business contact. Westerners new to the market may not realize that in Korea negotiations actually begin with your very first contact. Hence the critical importance of a proper introduction, referral or recommendation.

When introduced, expect a bow and moderate eye contact, often followed by a handshake. Respond with a slight bow before exchanging name cards. Receive your counterpart's card with both hands. Present your own card with the right hand or with the right hand supported at the elbow by your left hand. Study the other party's card, then place it in a quality leather card holder or on the conference table in front of you.

Forms of Address. Korean names normally consist of the family name first, followed by two (occasionally one) given names. Refer to your counterpart by his family name, as in 'Mr. Kim.'

To show respect to senior people, substitute his title for 'Mr.' For example, 'President Kim' or 'Director Park.' It is possible you will never use your local counterparts' given names.

Gift Giving. Gifts may be given at the beginning or the end of the meeting. Wrapping paper should be in pastel colors; bright colors are inappropriate. If you are meeting your counterpart at his office, bring a gift if you have just arrived from abroad. If invited to a Korean home, always bring a present.

Appropriate gifts include items typical of your own country or region as well as expensive cognac or whiskey. Present the gift with either the right hand only or with the right supported at the elbow with the left hand. The recipient will probably put it aside and open it later. You should receive a gift with both hands and open it later.

Wining and Dining. Entertaining and being entertained is an essential part of building a close relationship. For males, ritual drinking is a traditional way to get to know your counterparts. It is appropriate to drink heavily, even to get drunk. Alcohol may help to dissolve the stiffness and formality often encountered during business meetings. Drinking can be a good lubricant to a sticky negotiation.

Males who prefer not to drink alcohol can excuse themselves on grounds of illness or religious rules. They may, however, miss out on some opportunities to deepen relationships and learn more about their Korean partners. Women are not expected to drink, and are definitely not expected to get drunk. Not joining in the male drinking ritual could represent a handicap for women doing business in Korea.

Taboo behavior includes blowing one's nose at the dinner table. It is better to sniffle during the meal or better yet, leave the room and blow your nose out of earshot.

Chinese Negotiating Behavior

Opportunities for marketers abound in Greater China, especially in the PRC. The privatization trend continues, with state companies now accounting for less than a third of total national output compared with over half in 1990. Although legal transparency is still lacking, new regulations continue to gradually open the market. For example, foreign-invested companies may now own and control distribution networks. Beijing is also working hard to attract investment in the country's poor interior provinces.

Hong Kong remains a popular entry point for Western firms new to China, although the explosive growth of Shanghai is creating a serious competitor. The integration of the former British colony into the PRC is proceeding slowly. A 2001 survey by the Hong Kong Transition Project of people's attitudes before and after the handover showed that only 28 percent of those polled saw themselves as 'Chinese,' compared with 25 percent in June 1997. About two out of three describe themselves as 'Hong Kong Chinese' or 'Hong Kong people.'

Unfortunately, English-language proficiency in Hong Kong is deteriorating because instruction in Mandarin or 'putong hua' is now required in all schools there, along with the local dialect of Chinese. That means English is now a third language, almost always taught by non-native speakers. So you may soon need interpreters even in the Fragrant Harbor – quite a shock for Old China Hands!

Meanwhile, the risk for **Taiwan** is that it will not only continue to lose low-end manufacturing to the PRC, but also research and development. Taiwan is the third largest manufacturer of information technology products in the world, making more than half the world's laptop computers, monitors and modems. IT companies might prefer to keep their R&D work in Taiwan, but the lack of direct-flight connections with factories on the mainland makes things awkward.

Greater China. To understand Chinese negotiating behavior it's helpful to visualize three concentric geographic circles of business cultures. The outer circle consists of East and Southeast Asia: Greater

China, Japan, South Korea and the ethnic Chinese communities of the ASEAN region. Here business visitors will find many shared values, attitudes and beliefs alongside some significant differences in business behavior.

Inside that wider circle we find Greater China: the PRC (including Hong Kong, of course) and Taiwan, which share a larger number of similarities. And then there is the People's Republic itself, where – despite variations between north and south, between the coastal provinces and the interior, and (most obviously) between Hong Kong and rest of the country – it is possible to speak of a relatively homogeneous business culture.

Ru xiang sui su is an old Chinese proverb meaning, 'Enter village, follow customs.' Good advice for international marketers anywhere, but particularly good if you are planning to do business in Greater China.

***Guanxi* Rules!** The first culture shock for Western marketers trying to get started in Greater China is the relationship-focused, connections-oriented *guanxi* way of conducting business. This approach contrasts sharply with the deal-focused, task-oriented business cultures of North America, northern Europe and Australia-New Zealand. People in strongly relationship-focused cultures are not accustomed to doing business with strangers, so the first step is to cease being a stranger. If you are new to the China market and lack good contacts, you'll need to 'pull *guanxi*', that is, piggyback someone else's connections.

We might paraphrase that old proverb to read, 'Enter market, follow customs.' And the best way to enter the Chinese market is to do it the Chinese way: indirectly, using intermediaries and *guanxi*.

Language. Many business people speak English these days, but it's still wise to ask whether you will need an interpreter, especially in the PRC. When working on a major deal you may wish to hire your own interpreter rather than relying on one supplied by your local counterparts.

Building a Relationship. Developing rapport is a critical part of the overall negotiating process. Get to know your counterparts before starting to discuss business. Socializing over drinks and meals is a good way to build rapport.

Showing Respect. Younger people are expected to defer to older, higher-ranking persons. Hence young Westerners must be careful to show respect to older, more senior Chinese counterparts.

Maintaining Harmony. The Chinese regard displays of anger or impatience as infantile and lose respect for people who cannot retain a calm exterior under stress. So stay cool and try to avoid open confrontation at all cost. A false smile is preferable to an honest scowl.

'Face' Issues. Face has to do with self-respect, dignity, reputation. You can lose face by appearing childish or lacking in self-control – for example, by losing your temper. You can cause your counterparts to lose face by expressing sharp disagreement, embarrassing them, criticizing them in public or by showing disrespect. Causing serious loss of face can completely disrupt a promising business negotiation.

You can give your counterpart face by using polite forms of address and observing local customs and traditions. Giving face is an effective way build a solid relationship. If you make a mistake you may be able to save your face with a humble apology. And you can save the others' face by avoiding confrontation and allowing them a graceful exit from a difficult negotiating position.

Indirect Verbal Behavior. Especially in the north, Chinese are reserved and formal compared to people from more informal and expressive cultures such as North America, Australia and Scandinavia. To resolve major issues they rely much more on face-to-face meetings than on written communication or phone calls.

Chinese negotiators often employ indirect, vague, oblique language wherein the meaning is deliberately ambiguous rather than clear and explicit. They use circumlocutions and evasive language not to mislead, but to avoid offending people.

For example, many Chinese consider it offensive to reply to a request with a blunt 'no.' Often a Chinese negotiator offers a polite evasion such as, 'That will require further study' or 'That will be difficult,' instead. This kind of indirect, polite discourse may confuse negotiators from deal-focused cultures accustomed to more direct language.

Paraverbal Behavior. Chinese, especially those from the northern part of the country, tend to speak softly. They also avoid interrupting other people, since this would be rude. It is important for visitors from expressive cultures to avoid talking loudly and to wait patiently until their Chinese counterpart has finished speaking before saying their piece.

Another feature of Chinese paraverbal behavior is that laughing or giggling sometimes signals stress, nervousness or embarrassment rather than amusement.

Nonverbal Behavior. Accustomed to indirect eye contact, Chinese may misinterpret a strong, direct gaze as an attempt to intimidate or to convey hostility. China is a low-contact culture, with very little touching in a business situation. Chinese also use few gestures. Avoid abrupt gestures, arm-grabbing and backslapping. Maintain an arm's-length distance when possible and avoid physical contact other than the handshake.

Avoid pointing with your index finger. Instead, indicate direction with your whole hand. Striking the palm of one hand with the fist of the other is considered a vulgar gesture. It is rude to touch or move objects with your foot.

You know you have said something wrong when your Chinese counterpart responds by sucking air in audibly through his teeth. This equates to a gasp of dismay in European cultures. To recover, change the subject or restate what you said in a different, perhaps more indirect way.

Orientation to Time. The Chinese value punctuality and adherence to schedules. They expect the same of their foreign counterparts – especially potential suppliers.

Negotiating Style

Adapting Your Sales Presentation. In Greater China, avoid opening with a joke or humorous anecdote. This would show inappropriate informality. Take care not to over-praise your product or company. Instead, offer testimonials or articles written about your firm. In other words, let others praise your product and your firm.

Likewise, avoid making negative comments about your competitors. Rather, you may want to pass along critical comments about your competitors made by respected third parties. It is better to let others criticize your competitors and their products.

Bargaining Range. Chinese negotiators often bargain vigorously and expect their counterparts to grant major concessions on price and terms during the course of the negotiation. They may measure their success at the bargaining table by how far they are able to move you away from your opening offer. So wise negotiators always build enough margin into their opening offer to leave room for bargaining.

Bargaining Style. Be prepared for haggling. Make any concession with great reluctance, and only on a strict 'if ... then,' conditional basis, demanding something equivalent in return.

Ploys and Counter-ploys. Although Chinese negotiators generally mask negative emotions, they may on occasion display anger as a tactic. Public sector negotiators in the PRC sometimes plead the poverty of their country to obtain a lower price. They may also flatter you as an 'old friend.' Be aware that 'friends' are expected to help China by offering better terms.

Duration. Negotiations tend to last a long time, especially when doing business with a government entity or a public sector company. Decisions take time. For example, it took Volkswagen nine years to negotiate an agreement to build an automobile factory in Shanghai.

Role of the Contract. Many Chinese negotiators regard the final written agreement as less important than the strength of the relationship with you and your company. That's fine for them, but be sure to get everything in writing anyway. The Chinese may expect to renegotiate the contract if circumstances change. Be prepared for this, and remember that renegotiation of terms can work for both sides. If they want to reinterpret a certain clause in their favor, consider agreeing on condition they accept amending another important clause in *your* favor.

Legal Advisors. While you will of course dialog with your lawyers throughout the bargaining process, keep them somewhat in the background until towards the end of negotiations. Many Chinese regard the presence of lawyers at the bargaining table as a sign of mistrust.

Maintaining the Relationship. Between personal visits, stay in regular contact with your counterparts by phone and correspondence. Deal-focused Westerners often overlook this vital step in enhancing the business relationship.

Business Protocol and Etiquette

Meeting and Greeting. The dress code for men is a conservative suit, white shirt and tie, for women a suit or dress. State your name and company name and offer a greeting such as *ni hao ma?* ('How are you?') Expect a soft handshake and moderate eye contact. Avoid greeting your counterpart with a bone-crushing handshake. To show respect, shake hands first with the most senior person, then with the others. Some Chinese may bow or nod instead of shaking hands. Chinese bow from the shoulders rather than, as in Japan, from the waist.

Business Cards. Exchange cards with each person present. Be sure to bring a large supply of business cards. Have the text of your card printed in Chinese characters on one side. The exchange of cards is done using both hands while bowing your head slightly. When receiving your counterpart's card, take a moment to read it and then put the card away in a leather card wallet or place it on the conference table in front of you, across from the individual who gave it to you. Do not write on someone's name card in the presence of the giver.

Names and Titles. Address your counterparts by surname plus relevant title, never by given name or surname alone. Most Chinese have three names, each usually of one syllable. The family name comes first, followed by the personal names. Thus Mr. Lee Kwan Yew would be addressed as 'Mr. Lee.' On Chinese-language business cards the surname is printed first, but on cards printed in Western languages the order may be reversed. When in doubt, ask.

Especially in Hong Kong, people with non-Chinese personal names (e.g. 'John') may be comfortable using first names, but wait for your counterpart to suggest this move. If your family name is long or difficult to pronounce you may be addressed by your first name plus honorific, e.g. 'Mr. George' or 'Mrs. Mary.'

Meeting Behavior. Meetings begin on time; visitors are always expected to be punctual. With both Chinese and visitors, the highest-ranking person enters the meeting room first. Seating arrangements are important. The host sits with the most important guest to his right. The foreign visitor's side is expected to open the discussion.

Meetings in the PRC tend to be long, with frequent silences between monologues. Avoid interrupting the silences. Either side can call for a break or can end the meeting by suggesting the timing of the next session.

Gift Giving. Exchanging gifts is a key part of the business culture, contributing to developing *guanxi*. Wrap your gifts carefully and include a card. Do not use red ink for the card; in China a letter written in red ink indicates a relationship is about to be severed.

If you buy the gift at an upscale department store or boutique, have the store wrap it in their logo box and wrapping paper. Red is the best color for wrapping paper; avoid white and black, which are funeral colors. Consider bringing the gifts into China unwrapped to avoid problems with Customs officials.

Present and receive gifts with both hands. Never praise or say anything positive about the gift you present. Your gift will probably be set aside unwrapped and opened after you leave.

Either give a small gift to each person in the order they were introduced, or a large gift to the whole group. If you have a special gift for an individual, present it privately. Expect to exchange small gifts with your counterparts towards the end of your first meeting. More substantial gifts are appropriate to seal an agreement.

Traditionally, Chinese would politely refuse a gift the first time it was offered. Some older Chinese still follow this custom. In such cases, simply offer the gift a second time.

Expensive cognac or whiskey (boxed) are good choices, others are photo books, framed photos, ties, books, calendars and any item your country or region is known for. Avoid clocks, watches and anything in sets of four. The Chinese words for timepieces and the number four sound like the word for death. Giving fruit or simple food items would imply the recipient is poor and hungry.

Avoid giving wine unless you know the recipient enjoys it. Avoid scissors and letter openers, anything depicting a fox or a badger and items made in Asia.

Wining and Dining. Entertaining and being entertained is an essential part of building a close relationship with your counterpart. Table manners in most parts of the PRC tend to be somewhat more informal than in Hong Kong or Taiwan. Willingness to use chopsticks will be appreciated as a sign that you value Chinese customs. When asked what you would like to eat or drink, the best response is 'Whatever you are having.'

Seating arrangements at a meal reflect status and show respect. The guest of honor is seated so as to face the main entrance to the room. Twelve-course banquets can challenge even a robust appetite. To indicate you have eaten enough, leave a little food on your plate and place your chopsticks neatly on the chopstick holder.

Chopstick etiquette: Avoid leaving them crossed or standing upright in your rice bowl. Do not gesture, tap the table or spear pieces of food with them. Use the handle ends of the chopsticks to transfer food from the serving dish to your plate unless a serving spoon is provided.

Drinking at a meal is a serious ritual in Greater China. It is considered rude and selfish to imbibe alone: do not drink until you have offered a toast (e.g. *ganbei*) to others at the table. Although *ganbei* means 'bottoms up,' just taking a sip is all right. When you toast someone, raise your glass with both hands, to show respect, and make eye contact. When it is your turn to be toasted, nod and take a sip of your drink.

Women are not expected to keep up with the rounds of banquet toasts and are definitely not expected to get drunk. Males who prefer not to drink alcohol can excuse themselves on the grounds of health or religious objections.

You may be invited to one or more formal banquets, depending on the length of your stay. Have your local contact, your distributor or hotel help you reciprocate with an appropriate banquet before you leave China.

Hosting Chinese Visitors. Few Chinese enjoy big steaks or rare beef. Your counterparts will usually prefer Chinese food. A restaurant offering local specialties may be a good choice, but very often business visitors from China prefer a good local Chinese restaurant, if available.

9. Southeast Asia
Filipino Negotiating Behavior

Filipinos definitely share the basic values, attitudes and beliefs of their Southeast Asian neighbors. They are, after all, ethnically and linguistically related to the Malays of Indonesia and Malaysia. But 400 years of Spanish colonialism followed by nearly a century of quasi-colonial U.S. influence have added other important features to the culture.

It happened that Spain administered their colony for four centuries indirectly from Mexico City, so the Filipino business culture shows traits commonly associated with Latin America. More recently, the presence of so many Americans in the Philippines and the emigration of so many Filipinos to the United States have had an impact on the culture.

These days, visitors will find Filipinos relationship-focused, hierarchical and relaxed about punctuality and deadlines. They are also a warm and friendly people deeply concerned about maintaining harmony and what Filipinos call 'smooth interpersonal relations' or SIR.

Language. While there are over 70 languages and dialects in the Philippines, the national language is Pilipino, based on Tagalog. One legacy of the long U.S. presence is that most Filipinos engaged in international business speak fluent English. Visiting negotiators who use that language will have no more difficulty than they would in Singapore.

Those planning to set up an office, joint-venture or subsidiary should note however that it is becoming difficult to find competent English-speaking middle managers and technicians because so many have been recruited to work as expatriates abroad. English-language competence, high level of education and flexibility combine to make Filipinos sought-after as expatriates.

Making Contact. As in other Asian relationship-focused cultures, most Filipinos are reluctant to talk business with strangers who come without an introduction or recommendation. Attending a trade show or joining an official trade mission are proven ways to meet prospective customers, distributors and partners. Or have someone introduce you, preferably a person or organization that knows both you and the party you wish to contact. Banks, trading companies, law firms, consulting firms and embassy or consular officials are often tapped to provide introductions.

The First Meeting. Getting to know your counterpart is an essential prelude to discussing a deal. Especially with older Filipinos, expect most of your first meeting to be taken up with general conversation. Sharing a meal helps you get to know your local counterpart, so does playing golf.

Each time you re-visit the country, remember to take the time to update your Filipino partners on what's been happening and socialize with them before getting down to business again. Be aware of the importance of *pakikisma,* the Filipino term for togetherness and camaraderie.

Orientation to Time. The tropical climate, low level of industrialization and traffic gridlock in Manila all conspire to make punctuality problematic. When you call for an appointment at 10:00 a.m., your local contact may jokingly ask, 'Ah, you mean Western time or Filipino time?' Despite the generally polychronic attitude towards time, business visitors are expected to be reasonably punctual for meetings.

Verbal Communication. Indirectness is the rule. The ever-courteous Filipinos are so anxious to avoid offending others they strenuously avoid using the rude word, 'no.' They prefer indirect, diplomatic language. There are many ways of saying 'no' in Pilipino without actually saying it. Because your local counterparts are accustomed to vague statements and evasive language to avoid insulting others, they may take offense if you are overly frank and direct.

Another reason for Filipino indirectness is their strong desire to avoid *hiya,* meaning shame or embarrassment. They strive to avoid bringing shame or embarrassment on themselves or others, and phrasing a statement in a roundabout way is a good method to reduce this risk.

Status, Self-Esteem, and Showing Respect. As in other hierarchical societies, Filipinos accord high status to older people, especially older males. It is important to show appropriate respect to higher-ranking persons. Younger business visitors should defer to senior Filipinos, particularly when the latter are buyers or potential customers. As in the rest of Asia, the customer is king in the Philippines.

Like other Southeast Asians, Filipinos are sensitive to slights and issues of face. The traditional Filipino concern for face and self-esteem was reinforced by the Spanish obsession with honor and *amor-proprio,* meaning self-respect or self-esteem. Visiting business people should be sensitive to this concern when dealing with Filipinos of any rank or condition.

Harmony. Filipinos try hard to maintain smooth relations with others, even if things appear smooth only on the surface. For Western negotiators the easiest way to lose face and cause others loss of face is to display impatience, irritation or anger. A display of negative emotion disrupts the harmony of the meeting. Negotiators should be careful to maintain a calm exterior even when discussions are not proceeding as planned.

Paraverbal Communication. Most Filipinos speak rather softly and rarely interrupt another speaker. They may be startled by loud talk and are easily offended if interrupted in mid-sentence. Expressive Western visitors should avoid raising their voices and try not to interrupt their local counterparts during business meetings.

Nonverbal Communication. Filipinos often greet each other by quickly raising and lowering their eyebrows. Accompanied by a smile, this gesture signifies a friendly 'hello.' Two people of the same gender often hold hands in public; this usually indicates friendship. Indicate the number 'two' by raising your little finger and ring finger rather than the index finger and middle finger as in many Western cultures.

Pointing at people or objects with your index finger is impolite. If you ask directions on the street, rather than pointing, local people may respond by shifting their eyes or pointing the chin in the direction indicated.

It is rude to beckon someone by crooking your index finger. To call a waiter, raise your hand or extend your right hand and wave it in a palm-down scooping motion. Avoid standing with your hands on hips; this indicates anger, arrogance or a challenge.

Negotiating Style

Topics of Conversation. Good topics are family, food, culture, sports and Filipino history. Avoid discussing local politics, poverty, religion or corruption.

Making a Sales Presentation. Use plenty of visuals and handouts, especially with materials having to do with numbers. Avoid anything smacking of 'hard sell.' Think in terms of offering your product or service rather than selling it.

Bargaining Range. Many Filipinos enjoy bargaining, so remember to build some extra margin into your opening bid or quotation. Smart negotiators keep a good supply of bargaining chips in their back pocket for use in the end game.

Decision Making. Coming to a business decision is likely to take longer than in deal-focused Western cultures. Patience is a key asset for negotiators in this part of the world.

Business Protocol and Etiquette

Meeting and Greeting. Expect a gentle handshake accompanied by moderate eye contact. Except for the handshake and sometimes a light pat on the back, Filipinos avoid physical contact with people they do not know well. Intense eye contact such as would be appropriate in southern Europe or the Middle East is considered 'staring' in the Philippines and is likely to make local people uncomfortable.

The way you dress shows either respect or disrespect to your local counterparts. For men, a business suit with white shirt with tie or the 'barong tagalog' – the formal Filipino shirt worn outside the trousers – are all appropriate for the first meeting. After that you should be guided by your partner's dress code. Women should wear a dress, lightweight suit or skirt and blouse.

Names. Many Filipinos have Spanish-sounding given names such as Maria and family names like Cruz and Coronel. These names were adopted during Spanish colonial rule and do not indicate Hispanic ancestry. Many upper-class Filipinos follow the Spanish custom of having two surnames, their father's, followed by their mother's. If your Filipino counterpart invites you to use her or his nickname, do so and invite them to use yours in return. If you don't have a nickname, think about inventing one.

Titles. Titles are important in the Philippines. As in Latin America, professionals are often addressed by their family name preceded by their title, e.g. 'attorney de la Cruz' or 'engineer Martin.' People without professional titles are addressed with Mr., Mrs. or Miss followed by the surname. If the person has two family names, you need use only the first (father's).

Gift Giving. Exchanging gifts plays an important role in relationship-building. *Utang na loob*, meaning debt of gratitude for favors or gifts, is an important component of the glue that holds this relationship-focused culture together. Filipinos do not usually open a gift in front of others.

If invited to a Filipino home, bring flowers or chocolates rather than alcohol as a hostess gift. A gift of wine or spirits would imply that your hosts might not have enough beverages for their guests.

Wining and Dining. Unlike in Japan or Korea, over-indulgence in alcohol is considered ill-mannered. When eating, Filipinos often hold the fork in the left hand, using it to push food into the spoon which is held in the right hand.

Filipinos enjoy *bago'ong*, a salty, pungent paste made from fermented shrimp and used as a sauce and condiment. Visitors can impress their local hosts by partaking of this Southeast Asian specialty. Your hosts may also try to shock you with *balut*, an egg containing a fully-formed duck embryo. If you are not tempted by this purely Filipino delicacy, you can demonstrate your appreciation of local culture by declining with a gentle smile and a twinkle in the eye rather than with an expression of disgust.

When dining at someone's home, always leave a bit of food on your plate. This assures your hosts they have fed you well. A clean plate signifies you haven't had enough to eat.

Indonesian Negotiating Behavior

Indonesia's culture is complex due to the diversity of its demographic makeup. Its population of over 200 million, making it the world's fourth most populous country, includes Javanese, Bataks, ethnic Chinese and 300 other ethnic groups. It is also by far the largest Muslim nation. Business visitors find the culture relationship-focused, hierarchical and relaxed about punctuality and deadlines. Indonesian negotiators tend to be soft-spoken, friendly and polite.

Language. The national language is Bahasa Indonesia, similar to Malay. Perhaps because the country was colonized by the Dutch rather the British, English is not as widely spoken as it is in Singapore or Malaysia. So if you are meeting your local counterpart for the first time it would be wise to inquire whether an interpreter will be necessary.

If you plan to set up an office or subsidiary, keep in mind that English-speaking middle managers are often hard to find in Indonesia. To solve this problem many foreign companies recruit management in the Philippines where experienced managers fluent in English are easier to find.

Making Contact. Most Indonesian executives are uncomfortable talking business with people they do not know. Attending trade shows and official trade missions are good ways to meet prospective customers and partners. Another way is to have someone introduce you, preferably a person or organization that knows both you and the Indonesian party you wish to contact. You can also ask your bank or a trading company, law firm, consulting firm or embassy official to introduce you.

Relationship First. Getting to know your counterpart is an essential prelude to discussing a deal in Southeast Asia. Expect most of your first meeting to be taken up with general conversation. Sharing a meal helps you get to know your Indonesian contact, so does playing golf and going sightseeing. Each time you visit the market take time to make small talk and socialize with them before getting down to business.

Verbal Communication. One important way Javanese maintain harmony during vigorous negotiations is to employ indirect, 'polite' language. There are at least a dozen ways of saying 'no' in Bahasa without actually saying it. Because your local counterpart is accustomed to circumlocutions and evasive language to avoid insulting others, he may take offense if you are blunt and direct.

But beware of stereotyping in this complex culture. If you happen to be doing business with a Western-educated Javanese or an ethnic Batak of Sumatra, for example, you are likely to encounter a more direct approach to verbal communication.

Indonesians are embarrassed by elaborate expressions of gratitude. They seem to respond best to a simple 'thank you.'

Paraverbal Communication. Indonesians tend to speak rather softly and rarely interrupt another speaker. They may be startled by loud talk and are easily offended if interrupted in mid-sentence. Western visitors should avoid raising their voice or engaging in conversational overlap.

Indonesians may laugh or giggle when they are nervous or embarrassed. Be careful not to join in the merriment until you know exactly what the laughter is all about.

Nonverbal Communication. Expect a gentle handshake accompanied by moderate eye contact when meeting someone for the first time. While Europeans generally shake hands each time they meet and depart, this is not necessary at subsequent meetings in Indonesia. When in doubt just do as your counterpart does. Except for the handshake, Indonesians avoid physical contact with people they do not know well.

Intense eye contact is considered 'staring' in Southeast Asia and may make Indonesians uncomfortable. Also, if you wear sunglasses in Indonesia do remember to remove them when meeting a local person. Talking to someone from behind dark glasses is very rude in this society.

Because Indonesia is a Muslim culture the left hand is regarded as unclean. Avoid touching people, passing food, or offering your business card with your left hand. It is okay to sign a document with your left hand if you are left-handed, but remember to give it to someone with your right hand.

Pointing at people or objects with your index finger is impolite. If you need to point, close your (right) fist and aim it thumb-first in the direction indicated. To call a waiter, simply raise your hand the way you did in school. Or extend your right arm and make a scooping motion with your hand.

Orientation to Time. Indonesia is a cluster of islands straddling the equator. The tropical climate combined with the low level of industrialization may explain why time is viewed differently there. While foreign visitors are always expected to be on time, local business people march to a different tick of the clock. So if you are kept waiting don't take offense. That is especially true in Jakarta where the cause of the delay could be a monumental traffic jam.

Of course the problem might be a different kind of jam – namely *jam karet,* which means 'rubber time.' Time and schedules are flexible in the tropics. Like most of their neighbors in South and Southeast Asia, the Indonesians consider people and relationships more important than schedules and deadlines. For example, the meeting before yours might have lasted an hour longer than expected, and it is considered very rude to break off one meeting just to be on time for the next one.

Two practical tips regarding time and scheduling: Try to be punctual for your meetings and have plenty of reading material with you in case you have to wait for your local contact.

'Face' and Communication. This is a traditional, hierarchical, face-conscious society. Which means that Western negotiators may have trouble communicating with Indonesians. How to avoid causing loss of face? Avoid open confrontation at all costs. Avoid words or actions that might embarrass or shame someone. Never correct or criticize your Indonesian counterpart in front of others.

Higher-status people never apologize directly to people of low status. Domestic servants or manual workers are likely to feel acutely embarrassed by a formal apology from a superior. A smile and perhaps a small gift accomplishes the same result without the embarrassment.

No one wants to tell you bad news. If your local business partner delays telling you about a problem until it is too late to do anything about it, do not get upset. Remember that Indonesians are showing you respect by shielding you from bad news. You can solve this communication problem by developing a climate of trust with your local counterparts.

Hierarchy, Status, and Respect. The traditional culture accords high status to older people, especially older males. It is important to show appropriate respect and defer to higher-ranking persons. Younger business visitors should defer to senior Indonesians, particularly when the latter are buyers or potential customers.

Maintaining Harmony. Like other Southeast Asians, Indonesians are sensitive to slights and issues of face. For Western negotiators the easiest way to lose face and cause others loss of face is to display impatience, irritation or anger. Showing negative emotion disrupts the surface harmony of the meeting. Visitors are advised to maintain a calm exterior even if they are frustrated or angry.

Negotiating with Indonesians

Making a Sales Presentation. Take time to gauge the English-language capability of your audience before launching into your pitch. Use plenty of visuals and handouts, especially with materials having to do with numbers. Avoid anything smacking of 'hard sell.' Think in terms of offering your product or service rather than selling it.

Bargaining Range. Indonesians seem to love to bargain. Since you are likely to run into unanticipated cost factors, remember to build some extra margin into your opening bid or quotation. With negotiations often dragging on for months or years, your counterparts have a lot of time to keep chipping away at your initial position. Smart negotiators anticipate this and keep a good supply of bargaining chips in their back pocket.

Decision Making. The decision-making process takes anywhere from four to six times as long in Jakarta or Bandung as it does in Chicago or Copenhagen. Remember to pack a large supply of patience when you do business in this part of the world.

Contracts. Indonesians tend to regard their relationship with you as far more important then the boilerplate they signed. They usually prefer to sort out problems in face-to-face meetings rather than by calling a lawyer or by referring to the fine print in the written agreement. Of course you should get everything in writing to avoid later misunderstandings, but try to be sympathetic to your Indonesian partner's request to renegotiate some of the contract terms later.

Business Protocol and Etiquette

Dress Code. The way you dress can show either respect or disrespect to your counterpart. Because of the tropical climate men may find it uncomfortable to wear a suit. Nevertheless, do don a dark suit when meeting a high-level government official. For meetings in the private sector a long-sleeved white shirt and tie with neat trousers is appropriate for meetings in the private sector. Women should wear a modest dress, lightweight suit or skirt and blouse.

Names and Titles. While many Javanese have only one name, people of the middle and upper classes often choose a family name. These surnames typically end in 'o' as in Sukarno, Suharto and Subroto. If you are introduced to a male with the single name Budi, for example, you should address him as 'Mr. Budi.'

Do not be surprised if your local counterparts call you by your given name preceded by Mr., Miss or Mrs. That's why 'Mr. Bob' and 'Mrs. Linda' are frequently heard appellations in Jakarta.

Gift Giving. Unlike many other Asian societies, Indonesia is not a gift-giving culture. If you do give someone a gift do not expect it to be unwrapped in your presence.

Refreshments. At business meetings you can expect to be served tea or a cold drink. No matter how thirsty you may be, wait until your host has taken a sip before drinking. To do otherwise would be a sign of disrespect or poor manners.

Malaysian Negotiating Behavior

Malaysia is a diverse, multi-cultural, multi-ethnic society. Malays account for around 50 percent of the population, ethnic Chinese about 30 percent and ethnic Indians (mostly of South Indian origin), 8 percent. Non-Malay Bumiputeras and a small Eurasian element round out the mix.

Business visitors interacting with the public sector will deal mostly with Malays, while in the private sector both Chinese and Malays are active. Ethnic Indians are more often found in the law, medicine, and education professions. It is important to remember that all Malays are by definition Muslim, but not all Muslims are Malays.

Language. The national language is Bahasa Melayu but English is widely spoken, especially in the private sector. Visitors can usually conduct business without an interpreter.

First Meeting. Get to know your counterpart before discussing the deal at hand. Expect much of your first meeting to be taken up with general conversation. Sharing a meal helps you get to know your Malaysian contact, as do golf and sightseeing. Stick to small talk and general topics until your counterparts signal they are ready to talk business.

Malaysians signal their readiness by asking specific questions about your project, your company or the purpose of your visit. Each time you re-visit the market, always take the time to update your counterparts on what has happened since your last meeting, socialize with them before getting down to business.

Indirect Verbal Communication. Malaysians strive to maintain smooth interpersonal relations during vigorous negotiations by employing indirect, oblique language. Expect them to employ evasive language to avoid insulting others. For instance, Malaysians often avoid saying the word 'no,' which is considered offensive. Hesitation, silence, changing the subject or giving a vague, roundabout response are all polite ways of saying 'no' without actually saying such a rude word.

Reserved Paraverbal Communication. Most Malaysians are soft-spoken. Visitors should avoid raising their voice, engaging in loud, raucous behavior or interrupting people in mid-sentence. While accepted in expressive cultures, conversational overlap is considered offensive in Malaysia.

Some Malaysians giggle or burst out laughing when they observe a mishap, for example when someone slips and falls down. While in Western cultures laughing under such circumstances would be considered inappropriate, in Southeast Asian societies it is simply a spontaneous reaction to an awkward or embarrassing situation. No offense is intended.

Nonverbal Communication. All over the world body language sends very strong messages. Unfortunately, the meaning of certain nonverbal signals differ sharply from culture to culture. Visitors to Malaysia need to be aware of how their body language can be misinterpreted.

For example, intense eye contact is considered 'staring.' It makes many Malaysians uncomfortable, as does our conversing with someone when wearing dark sunglasses. Indoors or out, this is considered rude.

Like North Americans, northern Europeans, and East Asians, Malaysians prefer to stand and sit about an arm's-length distance from other people. Since Malaysia is a low-contact society, avoid touching people except for a gentle handshake. Backslapping and arm-grabbing are definitely out of place.

Malaysians use few gestures. They are likely to be startled or confused by sudden hand and arm movements. Using your index finger to point or beckon is impolite. If you need to point, close your (right) fist and aim it thumb-first in the direction indicated. To beckon a waiter, raise your hand or extend your right arm and make a scooping motion with the fingers of the right hand.

The left hand and the foot are regarded as unclean by both Muslims and Hindus. Avoid touching people or passing objects with your left hand. Likewise, avoid touching or moving any object with your foot, and do not cross your legs in such a way that the sole of your shoe faces someone.

Standing with hands on hips signals anger or hostility to Malaysians, while smacking your open palm with your fist may be misinterpreted as an obscene gesture.

Orientation to Time. Visitors are expected to be on time for meetings, while local counterparts are likely to be more relaxed. Traffic jams make it increasingly difficult to be punctual for appointments in Kuala Lumpur. The wise visitor schedules no more than two meetings per day: a recommended schedule is a meeting at 10:00 a.m. and another at 2:00 p.m.

Formality, Hierarchy, Status and Respect. This traditional culture accords high status to older people, people of high rank in organizations and to the Malay nobility. Younger business visitors should defer to senior Malaysians, particularly when the latter are buyers or potential customers. Politeness and formality in manners show respect to your counterpart.

'Face' Issues. Malaysians are sensitive to perceived slights. An easy way to lose face and cause others loss of face is to display impatience, irritation or anger. Showing negative emotion disrupts the harmony of the meeting and is interpreted as arrogance. Three tips regarding face:

- Avoid open conflict and confrontation during meetings, including words or actions which might embarrass or shame someone. For example, never correct or criticize your Malaysian counterpart in front of others.
- Overly-direct statements or remarks can easily offend Malaysians. Blunt speech may be interpreted as rude and ill-mannered behavior. Observe your counterparts' polite, indirect style of communication and act accordingly.
- 'Give face' to your counterparts by showing appropriate respect, for example by using the correct forms of address and observing local customs (See Business Protocol and Etiquette below).

Negotiating Style

Making a Presentation. Speak clearly and avoid slang, sports jargon, buzzwords and double negatives. Use plenty of visuals and handouts, especially with materials having to do with numbers. The 'soft sell' works better in Malaysia than the aggressive style favored by some Americans who are not used to doing business in Asia.

Bargaining Range. Many Malaysians love to bargain. Since you may run into unanticipated cost factors, remember to build some margin into your opening bid or quotation. Smart negotiators keep a few bargaining chips in their back pocket for the all-important end game.

Lawyers, Contracts, and Disputes. Malaysians prefer to resolve disputes in face-to-face meetings rather than via fax and e-mail. They rely more on relationships than on contract clauses to resolve business disagreements.

During the early stages of contract negotiations, it is wise to keep your lawyers somewhat in the background rather than at the bargaining table. To many Malaysians the presence of a lawyer indicates lack of trust.

Business Protocol and Etiquette

Dress Code. Because of the tropical climate, men may find it uncomfortable to wear a suit. Nevertheless, male visitors should don a dark suit, white shirt and tie when meeting a high-level functionary. For meetings in the private sector a long-sleeved white shirt and tie with neat trousers is appropriate. Women wear a modest dress, lightweight suit or skirt and blouse, being sure to cover the upper arms. Skirts should be at least of knee length.

Meeting and Greeting. Customs vary within this very diverse society. One common greeting in the business community is a gentle handshake accompanied by moderate eye contact. Here are two other practices:

- Malays (Muslims) may offer a graceful *salaam*. With a slight bow, extend one or both hands to lightly touch the other person's hands, then bring the hand(s) back to touch your heart.
- Indians may use the equally graceful *namaste* or *namaskaram* gesture, placing palms together vertically with fingertips just below chin level, accompanied by a slight bow or nod of the head. Male visitors should wait for Malaysian women to offer their hand. If no hand is offered, the polite male just smiles and exchanges verbal greetings.

Good topics of conversation include travel, sightseeing, business conditions in your country and food. Avoid commenting on local customs, politics or religion.

Exchanging Business Cards. With ethnic Chinese, exchange cards using both hands. With Malays and Indians, offer your card using your right hand with the arm supported at the wrist by the left. It is polite to study your counterpart's card for a few seconds before putting it away.

Names. The name game is as complex as the culture. Customs vary among Malays, Chinese and Indians. In general, address each person you are introduced to with his or her title and name. If the person does not have a professional, academic or noble title, use Mr. or Miss/Mrs./Madam.

Here are some culture-specific tips:

With a Malay name such as Abdul Hisham Hajji Rahman, Rahman is his father's name and Hajji indicates the father visited Mecca. He is addressed formally as Encik ('Mr.') Hisham, less formally as Abdul Hisham. If Encik Hisham has made the pilgrimage he may be addressed as Hajji Hisham. A Malay woman is addressed with *Puan* plus her name. Remember that if her name is Noor binti Ahmad, she is addressed as Puan Noor – Ahmad is her father's name.

Ethnic Chinese family names precede the two given names. For example, Li Er San is addressed as Mr. Li. If he gives his name as James Li, he may suggest you call him James, but wait for him to do so. Note: Since most Chinese wives do not take their husband's name, they should be addressed with 'Madam' plus their maiden name rather than 'Mrs.' plus the husband's name.

Indian names vary both by their religion and also by where their ancestors came from in India. Indian Muslim names are similar to Malay names. A South Indian Hindu named S. Nagarajan is addressed as Mr. Nagarajan since 'S' is the first initial of his father's name, while an Indian Hindu from the north named Vijay Kumar would be Mr. Kumar. His Sikh neighbor Suresh Singh is Mr. Suresh because the name 'Singh' is common to all male Sikhs.

Westerners are often addressed by their given name preceded by Mr., Miss or Mrs. So your Malaysian contacts may call you 'Mr. William', 'Mrs. Mary' or 'Dr. Robert.'

Titles. Titles are important in this rather formal, hierarchical society. Three common titles are Tun, Datuk (or Dato) and Tan Sri. Address Dato Abdul Hisham Rahman as 'Dato.' The king and the nobility are treated with great respect in Malaysia.

Refreshments. At business meetings you can expect to be served tea or a cold drink. If asked what you would like to drink, the polite response is, 'Whatever you are having.' Wait until your host has taken a sip before drinking.

Gift Giving. Gifts are normally exchanged only between friends. If you or your company already has a relationship with your Malaysian counterparts, gifts of food are good but avoid alcohol for Muslims and pork products for both Muslims and Hindus. If invited to a dinner or party, fruit, candy and cakes are acceptable gifts. A gift is normally not unwrapped in the presence of the giver.

Avoid giving knives, letter openers or clocks to a Chinese: sharp objects suggest the cutting off of a relationship, while the Chinese word for timepiece sounds like the word for death.

Singaporean Negotiating Behavior

The Republic of Singapore is unique in the world marketplace. Flourishing on a lush tropical island just a stone's throw from the equator, this modern city-state stands out as the world's only industrialized economy outside the Temperate Zone.

The Republic's economic success is due to many factors, especially hard work, frugality and effective government ... and air conditioning. Those who have worked under conditions of tropical heat and maximum humidity can appreciate the impact of climate on productivity and the work ethic. So the advent of cooled air certainly played a supporting role in Singapore's rapid rise to wealth.

The Languages of Business. Another important factor in Singapore's success as an entrepôt is its multilingual and multi-ethnic blend of Chinese (78 percent), Malays (15 percent) and Indians (6 percent). Most of the ethnic Chinese business people speak both Mandarin and English, the world's number one and two languages, respectively.

Fluency in Mandarin provides Singaporeans special access to the booming China market, while competence in English makes doing business easy for exporters, importers and investors around the world. In addition, the Malay connection is useful in the neighboring markets of Malaysia and Indonesia, while Singapore's diverse Indian community eases entry to the India market.

In brief, Singapore is a case study in how ethnic and linguistic diversity can contribute directly to a nation's economic success.

Business Culture. English-language competence is not the only reason Western negotiators find it easy to do business in the Island Republic. Growing convergence in business customs and practices is another. While the national culture continues to emphasize traditional Asian values such as the importance of family, concern for 'face' and respect for authority, Singapore's business culture is quickly evolving towards an international style with which globe-trotting executives are familiar.

Hundreds of European, American and Asian companies have found that Singapore's geographic position plus the familiarity of language and business customs make it the ideal site for their Asia/Pacific head-quarters. High costs in Hong Kong and Tokyo are driving more and more regional head offices to the Lion City.

Making Contact. The rapidity of change in business customs and practices has opened a generation gap within the Singapore business community. Local entrepreneurs and managers who are in their 50s and 60s tend to do business in a traditional, relationship-focused mode, while younger business people are usually more deal-focused. This is especially true of the many Western-educated managers in the Lion City.

With companies managed by younger men and women, although an introduction never hurts, you can usually save time by making direct contact. With more traditional companies, however, the indirect approach via a third party – using *guanxi* – is the route to go.

Verbal Communication. Although accustomed to speaking more directly than other Southeast Asians, Singaporeans still try to avoid answering questions or requests with a blunt 'no.' Nor does the word 'yes' necessarily mean your counterpart agrees with you. Unless spoken with emphasis, it may just be a way to avoid confrontation. Most Singaporeans dislike open conflict during a business meeting and readily resort to verbal evasiveness to avoid giving offense.

Avoid asking negative questions such as, 'Isn't my shipment ready yet?' If a Singaporean replies 'Yes,' he or she usually means 'Yes, it is *not* ready,' whereas most Westerners would take it to mean the ship-ment *is* ready to ship.

Some visitors perceive their Singaporean Chinese counterparts as overly aggressive because of the way they ask questions. For instance, 'You want this sample now or not?' may sound rude, but it simply means, 'Would you like to have a sample now?'

Singaporean English may vary in other ways. If your counterpart offers to 'send' you to the airport, that means he will pick you up at your hotel himself and drive you there. If he is cruising the streets looking for an empty 'parking lot,' he is seeking what Americans call a parking space.

Paraverbal Behavior. Most Singaporeans speak relatively softly. Loud talk is a sign of poor manners. A laugh or giggle at inappropriate times may signal embarrassment rather than amusement. Try to avoid interrupting people: conversational overlap is impolite.

Nonverbal Behavior. Expect a rather gentle handshake. Avoid responding with a bone-crushing grip. Men usually wait for a woman to offer her hand first.

When seated, be careful not to cross your legs in such a way that the sole of your shoe is pointed at someone. Do not touch or move objects with your foot. As in other parts of Southeast Asia, avoid beckoning someone with a crooked forefinger. The polite way is to extend your right arm palm down and make a scooping motion.

Negotiating Behavior. To conclude an important deal, expect to make a number of trips to Singapore over the course of several months. The pace of negotiations is slower than in more deal-focused business cultures. Visiting business people find Singaporeans polite but tough and persistent negotiators.

Business Protocol and Etiquette

Dress Code. The standard business attire for men is a long-sleeve white shirt and tie with dark trousers; for women a lightweight dress, suit or skirt and blouse. Most bankers, brokers, lawyers and some accountants wear suits, however. When meeting government officials, men should wear a suit (even though the official will be in shirt and tie) and should not remove the jacket until invited to do so.

Meeting and Greeting. Meetings usually start and sometimes end with a handshake. You can generally get down to business without elaborate rituals and hours of small talk, and you can expect your Lion City counterpart to be fairly punctual for meetings as well. Good topics for conversation are food, travel, sightseeing, history and business. Avoid discussing local politics, religion or sex.

Names and Titles. Avoid using first names until your Singapore counterpart suggests it. This is especially important when dealing with older or high-ranking people. Many Singaporean Chinese have a Christian given name in addition to their three Chinese names. When introducing two people, state the name of the more important or more senior person first, e.g., 'Chairman Lee, meet Mr. Jones.'

Exchanging Business Cards. These are called 'name cards' in Southeast Asia. After introductions, the visitor presents his or her card first, preferably with both hands but never with the left. The card should be handled with respect as it represents the person who gave it to you. Do not toss it casually onto the conference table, put in your back pocket, or write on it.

Gift Giving. Remember that when dealing with government officials, gift giving is taboo and that if they go to lunch with you they will insist on paying their share. Singapore officials have earned an enviable reputation for honesty and efficiency around the world.

For private-sector contacts the best choices are items your home country, region or city is famous for. Otherwise, picture books, expensive cognac or whisky or writing instruments are suitable.

Wining and Dining. Meals are a very important part of life in Singapore, and excellent cuisine is available all over the island. Singaporeans are extremely hospitable, and the island's famous cuisine is as delicious as it is varied. Two of the most famous local specialties are pepper crab and durian – the latter an 'aromatic' delicacy regarded by Southeast Asians as the King of Fruits.

Spouses are usually invited for dinner but not for lunch. Business breakfasts are becoming more common. Do not be surprised if your counterparts take their leave immediately after dinner: that is the local custom. Some Singaporeans tease visitors by pushing them to sniff the powerful odor of the durian. While the taste is quite bland, to most outsiders the scent is reminiscent of a clogged sewer.

Another famous specialty in Singapore is fish-head curry. Southern China contributed the fish head, India the basic curry sauce and Southeast Asia some of the spices. It is a fitting symbol of the unique Chinese/Malay/Indian potpourri that is Singapore.

Thai Negotiating Behavior

Thailand's customs, traditions and business behavior owe much to both China and India. In a sense the Thais form a bridge between the 'chopstick cultures' of Southeast Asia and the 'banana-leaf cultures' of South Asia. These diverse influences make Thailand a complex but delightful place to do business.

The Language of Business. Language is often the first problem business visitors encounter. Thailand means 'Land of the Free,' reflecting the country's unique status as the only Southeast Asian country which has never been colonized. One result is that relatively few Thais speak European languages. So while English-speaking negotiators rarely need an interpreter in former British colonies such as India, Sri Lanka, Singapore or Malaysia, it's a different story in Thailand.

That is why it is a good idea to ask whether you need to arrange an interpreter for the first meeting with your local counterpart. If you plan to set up an office or subsidiary, keep in mind that qualified English-speaking middle managers are hard to find in Bangkok.

Making Initial Contact. Most Thais are reluctant to talk business with people they do not know. That applies especially to any foreigner trying to sell them something. A good solution is to meet your prospects at a trade show or on a trade mission. Otherwise, arrange to be introduced – ideally by a person or organization of high status that knows both you and the Thai party. Failing that, see if you have a friend with a non-competing company already represented in Bangkok. If so, ask him or her to introduce you.

Other sources of introductions are your country's embassy, its chamber of commerce or bank, plus trading companies, law firms or consulting firms. The key point is that cold calls are unlikely to work in Thailand.

Maintaining Harmony. Once you have set up a meeting, the next cultural value likely to cause a problem is the importance of maintaining surface harmony during negotiations. Direct confrontation tends to disrupt the harmony of the meeting, so most Thais prefer indirect language.

A key Thai value is *kreng jai*, showing concern and consideration for the needs and feelings of others. Deal-focused Western visitors sometimes unintentionally offend by being too direct and by using pushy, hard-sell tactics.

A related value is *jai yen*, literally 'cool heart.' When the discussion gets lively, avoid raising your voice, displaying anger or openly criticizing your local partner. Maybe that's one reason Thais smile so much. They smile when they are happy, they smile when they are sad, they even smile when they are angry. Smiles and gentle words promote harmony; scowls and loud voices disrupt harmony.

'Face' Issues. Here are four proven tips for avoiding misunderstandings in this relationship-focused, face-conscious society:
- Avoid conflict and open confrontation at all costs.
- Avoid words or actions which might embarrass or shame someone, even unintentionally. For instance, never correct or criticize your Thai counterpart in front of other people. Remember that many Thais even feel uncomfortable if they are singled out for praise.
- Bear in mind that in this vertical culture, higher status people do not apologize directly to people of low status. Domestic servants or manual workers are likely to feel acutely embarrassed by a formal apology from a superior. A friendly smile and perhaps a small gift of sweets later accomplishes the same result without the embarrassment.
- If you have inadvertently offended someone of equal social status, such as a business partner, demonstrate humility. Smile and ask him or her to forgive your clumsiness. After that smile a lot and spend as much time together as possible. Building a strong personal relationship is the best way to avoid giving offense and to recover from causing loss of face.
- Thais do not like to tell you bad news. If your local business partner delays telling you about a problem until it is too late, do not get upset. Thais seem to feel they are showing you respect by shielding you from bad news. The way to bridge this communication gap is to develop a climate of trust with your local counterparts.

Hierarchies, Status, and Respect. Thais accord high status to older people, especially older males. It is important to show appropriate respect to senior, high-ranking persons – particularly if they are customers or government officials.

Time. Visitors from clock-obsessed cultures encounter another challenge: A very relaxed attitude to time and scheduling. The tropical climate and relatively low level of industrialization plus (in Bangkok) the permanent traffic gridlock all conspire to frustrate business people from rigid-time cultures. Some visitors go so far as to change hotels in Bangkok each evening so as to be closer to the next day's meeting site.

Like most of their neighbors in South and Southeast Asia, Thais consider people and relationships to be more important than schedules and deadlines. Your Thai contact may keep you waiting because he was caught in a traffic jam, or perhaps because the meeting before yours took an hour longer than expected. In the Thai business culture it would be unthinkable to break off an ongoing meeting in order to be on time for the next one.

Business Negotiating Style

Your Sales Presentation. Take time to gauge the English-language capability of your audience before beginning your presentation. Use plenty of visuals and handouts, especially with materials having to do with numbers. Avoid the aggressive 'hard sell' approach.

Meeting Behavior. Avoid overly long meetings, break up lengthy discussions with some social activities. Thais tend to be put off by 'all work and no play.' *Sanuk* or 'fun' makes hard work easier to take.

Bargaining Behavior. Be prepared for a certain amount of bazaar haggling. It's a good idea to add a 'comfort factor' to your opening offer in order to make room for some tactical concessions later on in price or terms. The decision-making process takes much longer than it does in more deal-focused cultures. Remember to bring a large supply of patience with you to the negotiating table.

Business Protocol and Etiquette

Dress Code. The way you dress can show either respect or disrespect. Men should wear a dark suit and tie when meeting a senior government official, while a long-sleeved white shirt and tie with neat trousers is appropriate in the private sector. Women may wear a modest dress, lightweight suit or skirt and blouse.

Meeting and Greeting. While a gentle handshake is appropriate when greeting Thai men, local women may employ the *wai* gesture: Both palms together at approximately chin level with the head slightly inclined. Raising the hands higher while bowing the head slightly more is appropriate when greeting a Buddhist monk. Thais avoid physical contact with people they do not know well.

Because the left hand is considered unclean, exchange business cards with your right hand only. To show special respect you may also present your card with the right hand, cupping your right elbow with the left hand. It is polite to present gifts the same way, but be aware that Thais really do not expect business gifts.

The Name Game. Thai surnames tend to be long, multi-syllabic and difficult for foreign visitors to pronounce. Fortunately, however, Thais are normally addressed by their first name preceded by *Khun,* as in 'Khun Somchai.' Similarly, visitors may be addressed as 'Mr. Jim' or 'Mrs. Linda.'

Paraverbal and Nonverbal Communication. Thais tend to speak softly and use almost no gestures. This reserved communication style caused an expat manager a problem a few years ago while interviewing job applicants in Bangkok. When several of the female candidates seemed confused during the interviews, the manager's local HR consultant gently explained that he was talking too loudly and using too many hand and arm gestures.

The women interviewees interpreted the loud voice to mean the manager was angry with them, and the arm-waving to mean he was mentally deranged. Which of course explained why he had so little success during the first round of interviews. After all, who wants to work for an angry, insane employer?

While Thais employ more eye contact than most Japanese, for example, intense eye contact such as would be appropriate in the Middle East or Latin America is considered 'staring' and makes many Thais uncomfortable.

The top of the head is considered sacred and should never be touched. Even if an adorable toddler waddles up to you with a toothy grin, restrain yourself from patting him or her on the head

The foot is even more unclean than the left hand. Visitors should never sit in such a way as to show the sole of their foot or shoe. Nor should we point to or touch an object with our foot or shoe. On a recent visit we observed the look of horror on a Thai hotel guest's face when a Western visitor shoved the Thai's suitcase aside with his foot to clear some space at the crowded registration desk.

Pointing at people with your index finger is extremely impolite. If you really need to point, aim your right fist thumb-first in the direction indicated. Or just jerk your chin in that direction. Likewise, beckoning to someone by crooking one's forefinger is rude. So to call a waiter it is better to simply raise your hand the way you did in school and make eye contact. Or extend your right arm horizontally, palm down, and make a rapid scooping motion with your hand.

A tall *farang* (European-type foreigner) should try to avoid towering over his or her local counterparts. It is polite to bend over a little to reduce any natural difference in altitude.

Personal Relationships. In general, you will find that developing and maintaining solid personal relationships with your local counterparts is the key to business success in Thailand.

Vietnamese Negotiating Behavior

During the late 1990s, Vietnam was regarded as a potential Asian Tiger. That Tiger was expected to really roar, but unfortunately it just didn't happen. Fueled by the lifting of the U.S. trade embargo in 1994, Vietnam did experience a burst of international business interest. Numerous foreign investment projects were initiated. But then frustration set in. The much-hyped 'doi moi' reform movement brought few practical results, so today Vietnam remains saddled with a communist economy closer to Cuba than to China. Its per capita GDP is less than half of China's, even less than that of most African countries. The result is that Hanoi's nine new luxury hotels remain mostly empty these days.

Once the economy does finally open up, however, international marketers and investors will certainly find opportunities in this large, potentially dynamic Southeast Asian country.

Language. A growing number of Vietnamese negotiators speak English, especially in the South. If you find it advisable to employ an interpreter, consider hiring your own linguist rather than relying on one supplied by your Vietnamese counterparts.

Get Introduced. Unless you represent a large, well-known company or have already met at a trade show or on a trade mission, the best way to make initial contact in Vietnam is to be introduced by a respected intermediary. Ask a bank, consultant, law firm, freight forwarder or your embassy to provide a formal introduction.

Build Relationships. As in the rest of Asia, developing rapport is a critical aspect of the overall negotiating process. Deal making is easier once you have established a personal relationship with your counterpart. Socializing over drinks and dinner is a good way to build rapport.

Orientation to Time. While Vietnamese are often late for a meeting, they do expect visitors to be on time. Showing up late indicates lack of respect for your local counterparts.

Hierarchies and Status. Younger, lower-ranking persons are expected to defer to older and higher-ranking individuals – and especially to senior government officials. Be prepared for a certain degree of formality in business meetings, although Vietnamese tend to relax as the relationship progresses.

Preserving Harmony. Vietnamese regard open displays of irritation, impatience or anger as rude behavior. They lose respect for people who cannot maintain a calm exterior under stress. Confrontation quickly disrupts harmony and leads to loss of face.

Face. You can cause your Vietnamese counterparts to lose face by losing your temper, embarrassing them, criticizing them in public, or expressing sharp disagreement. Causing loss of face can completely disrupt a promising business negotiation. On the other hand, saving your counterpart's face can contribute to the success of your negotiation. For instance, if you need to correct a Vietnamese negotiator's mistake, call for a break and diplomatically point out the error over a cup of tea. Your sensitivity to face will go a long way towards building a strong relationship with Vietnamese.

Verbal Communication. Vietnamese often employ indirect, vague, 'polite' language. For most Vietnamese, avoiding conflict and maintaining a pleasant relationship are far more important than mere clarity of meaning.

You may find the Vietnamese somewhat reserved and formal until you have built rapport. Especially in the early stages of the relationship you will accomplish far more with face-to-face meetings than with letters, faxes and phone calls. Frequent travel to Vietnam is a definite prerequisite to success in business there.

Paraverbal Communication. Vietnamese tend to speak more softly than many Westerners. They also avoid interrupting other people since conversational overlap is regarded as extremely rude behavior. Wait until the Vietnamese negotiator has finished speaking before chiming in.

A laugh or a giggle frequently signals embarrassment or stress rather than amusement, so avoid joining in the general merriment at a meeting until you understand just what is going on. Avoid raising your voice at the bargaining table: A loud voice indicates anger or childishness in Southeast Asia.

Nonverbal Communication. Expect a gentle handshake and indirect eye contact. Strong, direct eye contact may be misinterpreted as an expression of hostility. A knuckle-crunching handshake is considered rude and offensive.

Body language is restrained: Vietnamese use few hand gestures. They may be startled or confused by wide, expansive gestures and arm waving. Vietnam is a low-contact culture so expect little touching. Avoid arm grabbing and backslapping.

Business Negotiating Style

Sales Presentations. North Americans, Australians and some other Westerners often start presentations with a joke or humorous anecdote. In Vietnam this approach is inappropriate. Try not to overpraise your own product or company – let your brochures and testimonials speak for you. By the same token, avoid badmouthing your competitors. Instead, pass along to the Vietnamese clips of any critical articles that have been published about the competition.

Remember to hand out copies or outlines of your presentation in advance. Use visual aids wherever possible, especially where numbers are concerned. Check frequently to see whether your counterparts are following the presentation.

Bargaining Range. Vietnamese negotiators tend to bargain vigorously and very often expect their counterparts to grant major concessions on price and terms. It sometimes appears that they measure their success at the bargaining table by how far they are able to move you away from your opening offer. Counter this tactic by building sufficient margin into your initial bid. Always leave yourself room for maneuver, and squirrel away some bargaining chips for the end game.

Making Concessions. Be prepared for some spirited horse-trading and bazaar haggling. Take great care to make any concession conditional – always demand something of equal value in return. Give in to any demand with extreme reluctance and only after lengthy hesitation. This is the one and only occasion during the negotiation process in Vietnam when you should let your face show some negative emotion. It is okay to show how painful that last price concession was.

Expect the Vietnamese side to withhold any major concession until the end game while at the same time they continuously push you to concede point after point. Just keep smiling and ignore any outrageous demand. Alternatively, keep smiling while you make an equally outrageous demand of the other side. Be patient, stay cool ... and keep smiling.

Decision-Making Behavior. Decisions are made by top management. High officials and private-sector executives are very busy, so decisions almost always take time. Larger private-sector firms are often headed by 'retired' military officers; here again decision-making is slow. Some smaller entrepreneurial firms act more quickly.

Role of the Contract. Don't be surprised if your Vietnamese partner contacts you a few weeks after the signing ceremony with a request to renegotiate key parts of the agreement (such as price, for example). Vietnamese expect that because of their close relationship you will agree to discuss changes in the contract any time conditions change.

Business Protocol and Etiquette

– When meeting with senior government officials men should wear a dark suit and a conservative tie. For other business meetings a long-sleeved shirt and tie for men and a conservative dress or skirt and blouse for women are appropriate attire.
– Receive your counterpart's business card with both hands, scan it carefully and then put the card away in a leather card case or place it on the table in front of you. Present your own card with your right hand or with both hands.
– Vietnamese names follow the Chinese pattern. If you are introduced to Nguyen Van Tuan, for example, Nguyen is the family name and the others are given names. Visitors should address Vietnamese by their family name – and title, if any.
– Vietnam is a gift-giving culture. A good choice would be an expensive branded cognac or whisky. Other ideas are items typical of your region or tasteful logo gifts. Present the neatly wrapped gift with both hands. The recipient will probably put it aside and not open

it until after you have left. When you are given a gift, accept it with both hands and a smile, but open it later.

– Entertaining and being entertained is an important part of building an effective relationship with your local counterpart. The major hotel restaurants in Saigon and Hanoi offer a selection of Chinese, French and local cuisines. Finding a good restaurant is more of a challenge outside the major cities – rely on local advice.

Maintaining the Relationship. Budget plenty of time as well as travel and communication expense in order to stay in close contact with your Vietnamese partners. Frequent visits to the market are essential.

Myanmar Business Negotiating Behavior

Myanmar, like Thailand, forms a cultural bridge between the ancient cultures of China and India. So business visitors with experience in those two markets will find familiar values, attitudes, beliefs and behaviors. Unlike Thailand, however, Myanmar has been isolated for decades from the rest of Asia and the world, so negotiating business there presents special challenges.

The People. About 70 percent of the 45 million people are Burmese. Among the numerous minority groups are the Shan, Karen and Arakanese, with ethnic Chinese and Indians accounting for about one percent each. Just as the Malays of Malaysia are defined as Muslims, most Burmese identify themselves strongly with Buddhism. Like Sri Lankans, Thais, Cambodians and Laotians, the Burmese follow the Theravada or Hinyana stream of Buddhism.

Key Values. Burmese are very proud of their ethnicity; many of them tend to look down on South Asians, Chinese, and other foreigners to the extent these outsiders behave in an 'un-Burmese'way. The values, beliefs and behavior encompassed by 'Burmeseness' (*Bahmasan chinn*) include showing great respect for elders, being able to recite from memory important passages of Buddhist scriptures and to converse in idiomatic Burmese. The people of Myanmar also have a preference for reserved and indirect speech as well as modesty in dress and manners.

Another key value is *ko chinn sar-nar-hmu*: a strong feeling of empathy and deep consideration for the feelings of others. Friends (including 'business friends') are expected to be sympathetic and empathetic in times of difficulty. Failure to show empathy is very likely to disrupt your business relationships.

Language of Business. Due to Burma's earlier history as a British colony, English used to be taught from kindergarten through university. In the 1960s however English instruction in the primary schools was swept away in a tidal wave of nationalism and xenophobia. Since the 1980s teaching English has made a comeback, so younger business people and most government officials speak it with some fluency.

Making Contact. As in most parts of Asia you are expected to approach potential business partners indirectly, via intermediaries such as your embassy, law firms or consultants. A direct approach would mark you as un-Burmese and perhaps undesirable as a partner. Since most of the economy is state-run, you will probably interact with government officials. Ministries are divided into corporations and directorates: the former deal in products, the latter in services. Corporations are headed by Managing Directors, directorates by Director Generals. The next highest rank is General Manager. Ministers sometimes attend meetings.

Relationships. Success in business depends on developing solid social relationships with your local partners. Plan to spend considerable time outside of office hours building rapport.

Verbal Communication. One reason Burmese value indirectness is to avoid imposing on others or causing loss of face. The important term *ah-har-hmu* refers among other things to the desire to avoid offending people or troubling them unduly. The result is that business visitors are likely to encounter indirect, evasive and roundabout language on a regular basis. People who are blunt are considered un-Burmese, crude and uneducated. 'Yes' often means 'I understand' rather than indicating agreement.

Few older Burmese say 'thank you' for favors done or 'sorry' when they make mistakes. To show that you are sorry, say 'forgive me' or explain that your mistake was unintentional. To express an apology nonverbally, give a small gift or do the person a favor. Burmese who are quite proficient in English are more likely to use the polite words and phrases.

Hierarchies and Status. As is the case in most of Asia, age and seniority are much respected. Remember to pay most of your attention to the senior person present, as defined by age and rank within the company or organization.

Nonverbal Communication. Burmese smile often, sometimes to cover discomfort or embarrassment. Body language is very reserved;

people tend to speak softly and use few gestures. The left hand is considered unclean; use only the right hand to pass objects to others.

Orientation to Time. Visitors are expected to be on time for meetings, but officials are likely to keep you waiting. Burmese tend to be relaxed about punctuality, schedules and deadlines.

Negotiating Style. Because foreigners are mistrusted you will probably need considerable time and repeat visits in order to reach agreement. In most cases decision-making is a slow process involving consensus-seeking; the final decision is made at the top. Business negotiations in Myanmar are conducted face-to-face.

Business Protocol and Etiquette

Dress Code. For men, a long-sleeved shirt and tie for private-sector meetings, lightweight suit when meeting senior officials. Women should dress modestly, usually in a suit, dress or skirt and blouse.

Names and Titles. Burmese names may cause problems for foreigners, especially since it is not uncommon for people to change their names. The traditional system is to name a child after the day of the week he or she is born on. It is very important to employ the correct honorific when addressing a Burmese. A working adult male named Myo Nu is addressed as U Myo Nu, an adult woman named Maung San would be Daw Maung San. The proper honorific for a male teacher or boss is Saya, for a woman Sayama.

Meeting and Greeting. People in Myanmar do not generally shake hands, but may do so with foreign visitors. It is a good idea to wait until a hand is offered. If not, a polite nod and smile is appropriate. Business cards are exchanged at the beginning of the meeting, using the right hand.

Meeting Behavior. Expect your first meeting to be primarily a 'get-to-know-you' session; serious business will be discussed at subsequent meetings.

Gift Giving. Good choices for business gifts include tasteful writing instruments, diaries and calendars. Once you know your counterparts, golf balls, cigarettes and good cognac or whisky are other possibilities. If the recipient politely refuses your gift, smile and insist until the gift is accepted. Gifts are not normally opened in front of the giver.

Appropriate hostess gifts include fancy fruit, chocolates and other sweets. Remember to remove your shoes before entering a home. Avoid giving knives, letter openers or scissors: in Myanmar cutting instruments symbolize the severing of a relationship.

Wining and Dining. Generally only Westernized Burmese drink alcohol. Most business entertainment is done over dinner (rarely at lunch or breakfast) in upscale hotels, and is relatively formal. A Chinese restaurant is often the best choice. Burmese usually expect to be coaxed repeatedly to take a second serving. Few people in Myanmar eat pork or beef.

10. South Asia
Bangladeshi Negotiating Behavior

Western business people have tended to dismiss the market potential of this large South Asian nation ever since Henry Kissinger called it an 'economic basket case' in the mid-1970s. But despite its poverty, profitable opportunities still exist for exporters, importers and investors.

Most market potential is concentrated in textiles – by far the country's most successful industry – so manufacturers of textile machinery and supplies should be looking for export and joint-venture investment opportunities.

But poverty is not the only deterrent to commercial interest in Bangladesh. Bureaucratic red tape, official corruption as well as major differences in business customs and practices create invisible barriers to trade. Here are some key elements of Bangladeshi business culture:

Scheduling. Avoid making appointments during or near Islamic holidays, especially Ramadan, a month-long 'moveable feast' whose dates vary widely from one year to the next.

Making Contacts. Your embassy, bank or consulting company should be able to put you in touch with interested local parties. The right contact for you is one who knows how to cut through the jungles of red tape without having to pay *bakhsheesh,* the local term for a bribe.

Building Relationships. This includes relationships with government officials. The state controls most of the Bangladesh economy with a heavy hand, which can cause endless frustration for business people. Fortunately, South Asian officials tend to be more accessible to foreign businessmen than is the case in some other parts of Asia. However, many foreigners bungle the chance to establish effective relationships with the public sector. They unthinkingly adopt a patronizing tone with Bangladeshi officials because of the country's poor socio-economic condition. This is a major faux pas. It is important to show appropriate respect when meeting with government officials, who enjoy very high status in the Bengali culture. (See the case, 'Negotiating with a Government Minister in Bangladesh' in Part I of this book.)

Verbal Communication. Your counterparts may be reluctant to say 'no' bluntly and may often avoid telling you bad news. The solution to these problems is to probe: patiently asking one question after another.

Nonverbal Communication. Bangladeshis avoid touching people they do not know well. As in other Muslim countries the left hand is unclean, as are the feet and shoes. Remove your shoes before entering a home or religious area. The common North American and Western European 'thumbs up' gesture is considered obscene, as it is in much of West Asia (the Middle East).

Orientation to Time. Pack an extra supply of patience when visiting Bangladesh. Poor infrastructure, frequent natural disasters and a relaxed attitude to scheduling combine to frustrate people accustomed to quick response and prompt deliveries.

The country's Islamic heritage is evident in attitudes towards time and scheduling. On one memorable flight from Chittagong to Dhaka in a rickety old Fokker, the Bangladeshi captain frightened some of the foreign passengers when he announced, 'Despite this monsoon rainstorm we will land at Dhaka airport shortly, God willing.'

Those of us familiar with the culture knew the pilot was simply translating the pious phrase *Insh'alla* into English. However, the elderly North American woman sitting in front of us understood that our captain wasn't sure we would make it, and she promptly fainted.

Business Negotiating Style

Bargaining Behavior. The Bengalis are a friendly, hospitable people who enjoy the give and take of a lively bargaining session. Expect your negotiations to take more time than they would in deal-focused cultures. It is important to keep a smile on your face even when discussions become a bit heated.

Decisions. In most Bangladesh businesses, all important decisions are made by the managing director, who typically is unwilling to delegate any of his authority. When this person is overburdened or 'out of station' your urgent fax or email is likely to go unanswered.

Business Protocol and Etiquette

Dress Code. For the first meeting with potential customers in the private sector, men wear a lightweight suit during the cooler months and a long-sleeved shirt and tie in the hot season. When meeting senior government officials wear a dark suit, white shirt and tie to show appropriate respect. Women should avoid sleeveless blouses and short skirts; modest dresses, suits and pants are appropriate.

Meeting and Greeting. Expect to shake hands with most men but wait for a woman to offer her hand. Some Bangladeshis prefer the *namaste* greeting, with both hands placed together at chest level with finger tips pointing upwards and accompanied by a smile and nod of the head. Cards are exchanged at the start of the meeting, using the right hand only.

Conversation. You will probably start talking business after a few minutes of small talk concerning your flight and hotel. Good topics for conversation include food, travel, sightseeing and your (favorable) impressions of Bangladesh. Avoid mention of poverty, politics and religion.

Meeting Behavior. During meetings with senior government officials, be ready for anything. Assistants and secretaries rush in with papers to be signed, incoming phone calls punctuate your carefully rehearsed presentation, friends and relatives drop in for a gabfest. The proper response is to stay calm, avoid showing impatience. While such behavior would be considered rude in monochronic cultures, it is normal meeting protocol throughout South Asia.

Gift Giving. Good choices include items your country or region is know for, quality pens, calendars, picture books and other modest gifts. Since 90 percent of Bangladeshis are Muslim, avoid gifts of alcoholic beverages as well as representations of dogs. Showing photos of your pet hound will not endear you to your local counterparts.

Good hostess gifts are chocolates and other sweets, including local products.

Wining and Dining. Few Bangladeshis drink alcohol or eat pork products. Most business meals are taken at dinner; business breakfasts are unusual.

Indian Negotiating Behavior

Marketers targeting India should be alerted to two recent developments. First, Bombay is now Mumbai and Madras has become Chennai. Second, the ongoing reform process has indeed brought some further improvements in terms of openness – but visitors must not imagine that doing business in India is now a breeze.

You will encounter a culture that is still heavily regulated, along with being strongly relationship-oriented, hierarchical in social interaction and polychronic in time behavior. Regarding the latter, it helps to know that in Hindi *kal* means both 'yesterday' and 'tomorrow.' That makes *kal* (pronounced 'cull') an apt symbol, because India is a true land of the future perpetually hamstrung by bureaucratic overregulation.

Red Tape. The world's second-most populous country with a population of over one billion, India now boasts some 150 million middle-class consumers. That makes India a powerful magnet for marketers and investors. Unfortunately, regulatory obstructionism continues to present obstacles for foreign business visitors, who regularly get tangled up in the ubiquitous red tape.

Old India Hands will tell you there are four keys to success in this enormous market:

1. Patience.
2. Finding the right local partner.
3. A basic grasp of this country's complex business customs and practices.
4. Patience!

Orientation to Time. Patience is especially important when dealing with officialdom. As we saw above, time has a different meaning in India. Taking the linguistic example a step further, *kal-kal* means 'the day before yesterday' as well as 'the day after tomorrow.' Minutes just do not count for much in this polychronic (fluid-time) culture.

Meeting with a senior government official? Prepare to be kept waiting half an hour or more without the courtesy of an apology. Nor should you be surprised if your important meeting is interrupted every few minutes while the harried official across the desk takes phone calls, signs piles of documents and receives impromptu visitors.

It would be a mistake to interpret this behavior as rude or reflective of sloppy work habits. Clocks in South Asia simply tick to a slower beat. It's a question of climate and culture: the closer a country is to the equator, the more relaxed is its time behavior. One solution is to carry a large briefcase stuffed with overdue expense reports and use that waiting time as an opportunity rather than a problem.

Connections. The right local partner will have the connections to reduce – but not eliminate – those frustrating delays. But avoid setting your hopes too high. You'll need a basic knowledge of the business culture in order to find the right partner and to enable you to work effectively with partners, clients, customers and suppliers.

Communication. India's billion-plus people speak 325 different languages not including dialects. The most widely spoken tongue is Hindi, used by less than 35 percent of the population. But there are 14 other official languages, some of them with several hundred million speakers. For instance, more people speak Bengali in India than speak Russian worldwide. Only about 2 percent speak fluent English, but those two percent include most of the commercial elite you are likely to interact with.

But watch out! Indian English is sprinkled with local terms which may confuse visitors. If you hear your partner referring to 'a lack of rupees' he may be talking about a *lakh* of rupees, which means 100,000 of them. And if your distributor shocks you by sayings she has just 'fired' her assistant, that just means the employee got a verbal reprimand.

Relationships and Trust. In most of the world's business cultures people trust foreigners much less than they do their co-nationals. In South Asia, strangely enough, the situation is reversed. Most Indian and other South Asian business people we know seem to trust foreigners, especially Westerners, far more readily than they do their own fellow citizens. This unusual cultural trait gives Western business people an important advantage when it comes to market entry.

Equally counter-intuitive, Westerners also often have an easier time getting appointments with senior government officials. One young U.S. manager we know, an expatriate with two assignments in New Delhi, ascribed his (modest) success in the Indian market largely to the numerous red tape-cutting personal meetings he was able to arrange with high-level officials, including one with the prime minister.

The Importance of Family. Any country's business culture reflects the basic values of the society. In India one such value is the importance of the family, which helps explain the fact that almost all businesses from Chandigar to Calcutta are family-run businesses.

Religion, Hierarchy, Status, and Caste. Hinduism is the majority religion, Islam and Sikhism are significant minorities. Other beliefs found in this cultural mosaic are Christianity, Buddhism and several forms of animism.

Intimately related to Hinduism is the concept of caste. Hindus belong to whichever caste they are born into. They cannot move up the caste ladder by getting a Ph.D., by getting elected to high office, or by becoming a millionaire. Some 14 percent of Hindus fail to qualify for even the bottom-most rung of the caste ladder. These are the untouchables, formerly known as *harijans*, currently called *dalits*.

Some years ago a *dalit* named Jagjivan Ram was the Minister of Defense and the second-most powerful political figure in the country. In New Delhi he was treated with all the outward signs of respect due his exalted status. But whenever he returned to his native rural village Jagjivan Ram was treated by his upper caste neighbors as just another untouchable, a social outcast. Culture changes at a glacial pace ... even in a torrid climate like India's.

The ancient tradition of caste is an extreme example of status distinctions, and it is formally illegal in modern India. But its continued existence nevertheless shows the importance of social hierarchies in this diverse South Asian society. Youngsters are expected to defer to elders; in direct contrast to American practice, white hair confers status. Visitors should be sensitive to differences in age and rank.

Bakhsheesh. Also called 'speed money', official bribery is unfortunately an integral part of the Indian business culture. Nonetheless, visiting business people would be well advised to avoid making payments which would be illegal in their own country or in India. Because Westerners often have an easier time getting in to see higher-level bureaucrats, one way to get things done without bribery is to cultivate relationships with key officials.

Let's cite the example of a Western expat manager who urgently needed a hard-to-get permit from a senior official in New Delhi, a permit essential to his business's success. He fought his way through crowds of equally desperate Indian petitioners to the official's desk. When the harried director looked up he suddenly began to smile and exclaimed, 'Ah, how nice to see you again! That dinner party last month was truly delightful. My regards to your wife. Now, what can I do for you?' Twenty minutes later the manager left the office, permit in hand.

Negotiating Behavior

Hierarchical Management Style. Try hard to meet as early as possible with the top boss, who is almost always the ultimate decision-maker in an Indian company. The CEO is often swamped with work and frequently 'out-of-station', so decisions take time.

Verbal Language. Although certainly less indirect than Japanese negotiators, many Indians are reluctant to say 'no' when a negative response is called for. Instead they may hint, delay giving an answer or simply ignore a difficult issue entirely. As with other aspects of Indian business behavior, however, there is a generational difference. You are likely to find that many younger Western-educated executives are more direct.

Since you rarely hear polite words such as 'please' and 'thank you' in conversation, you might perceive English-speaking Indians as rude. But that is because in Hindi and other Indian languages, politeness is expressed by the use of certain grammatical forms rather than separate words. And since most Indians learn English from non-native speakers of 'standard' English, they tend to unconsciously translate from Hindi, Bengali or other local tongue. Most Indians interact very courteously with people – especially with Western visitors.

Nonverbal Signals. Tilting or wobbling the head from side to side can mean 'Yes, I agree' or 'Yes, I hear you' or sometimes 'Maybe.' The head tilt does not necessarily mean agreement, so ask indirect questions to verify the situation. Rotating the right hand at the wrist while waggling the fingers is a gesture usually indicating indecision, commonly translated as 'Perhaps' or 'I don't know.'

Bargaining Range. Indian negotiators are famous for making opening bids far from their real bottom line. So it is a good idea to build plenty of bargaining room into your initial price quotation. Your local counterparts will usually assume you have a fat margin and hence expect you to make substantial concessions. If you can't, some Indian negotiators will conclude you don't really want to do business with them.

Bargaining Style. Here again you might encounter a generational difference. Older Indians seem to dearly love bazaar haggling while some younger managers consider it an outmoded way to try to reach agreement.

Contracts and Lawyers. Verbal agreements are not binding here, as they are in some parts of East and Southeast Asia. Detailed written contracts are the norm. Lawyers generally have lower status than in most Western cultures.

Getting Paid. When exporting to India, it is a good idea to demand payment upfront or to require an irrevocable letter of credit confirmed by a reliable bank in your home country.

Business Protocol and Etiquette

Scheduling Meetings. Avoid arriving during major religious holidays such as Diwali or Deepawali. Try to avoid the monsoon season as well; traffic can be snarled for an entire day in Mumbai and New Delhi during spectacular downpours. Many Indian executives do not arrive in the office until mid-morning, so avoid making appointments before 10:00 a.m. in the morning. Schedule your first afternoon meeting no earlier than 2 p.m.

Meeting and Greeting. For men, when meeting government officials or for the first meeting with potential customers, a dark suit is appropriate attire. For other meetings, during the hot season a short-sleeved shirt with neat trousers is acceptable. Women should wear lightweight conservative clothing, showing as little skin as possible. Suits, dresses and skirts and blouses are all acceptable. Cotton is good in the summer months, silk in the cooler months.

You may be greeted with either a handshake or the graceful *namaste* or *namaskar* gesture. Return the latter greeting by joining your palms together just below the chin, finger tips up, as though praying, while inclining your head forward in a slight bow or nod. Senior officials as well as many Indian women generally prefer the *namaste* gesture to the handshake.

Business cards are exchanged – not necessarily at the beginning of the meeting – without elaborate ceremony. Only the right hand is used to present and receive cards. (In fact, the right hand is the *right* [correct] hand in all business and social interaction throughout India and the rest of South Asia, where the left hand is considered unclean.)

One special and charming South Asian custom is the garlanding of visitors. Business visitors often wonder what to do with the garland after it has been draped around their neck. The appropriate response is to smile in thanks, remove it gently as soon as the flash bulbs stop popping and carry it in your hand until your hosts relieve you of the fragrant burden.

Name and Titles. Until you know your counterparts well, address them with surname plus title or honorific, e.g. Dr., Mr. or Mrs. Wadia. With senior government officials always use formal titles no matter how long you've known them. With others, wait until specifically invited before using first names.

With northern Hindus given names come first, followed by the family name; for example, Mr. Kishan Babu Lall. This gentleman might also be called K.B. Lall. A southern Hindu man named Nagarajan whose father's name is Vishnu would be called V. Nagarajan. Sikh men use a given name followed by Singh; with women 'Kaur' follows the given name.

With Muslims, names tend to be rather complicated for Westerners. The safest approach is to ask the person how he or she wishes to be addressed.

Meeting Behavior. Visitors should aim to arrive on time, but your counterpart is unlikely to be offended if you arrive within 15 minutes of the scheduled time. When meeting with government officials, you are expected to be punctual but you are likely to be kept waiting. Do not be surprised if 'your' meeting with an official is interrupted repeatedly by phone calls, secretaries bearing papers to be signed and drop-in visitors.

Expect to spend at least five minutes chatting before talking business, although some younger Indian business people get down to business almost immediately. Good topics are local food (avoiding any mention of pork or beef), sightseeing, Indian culture, sports, music, history, Indian films and novels, and how much you enjoy traveling in India. Avoid talking about politics, religion, local poverty and disease as well as the caste system unless you know your counterparts very well.

Nonverbal Behavior. Males shake hands with other men when meeting and again when they part. Never touch a women except to shake hands – if she offers her hand, that is, since many Indian women prefer the *namaste* gesture. Except for the handshake avoid touching your local counterparts.

It is extremely impolite to place your foot on a chair or table, or to touch a person or object with your foot. If you need to point at someone, use your whole hand, palm up, rather than your index finger. Beckoning should likewise be done only with the whole hand (this time palm-down), waving your fingers as though scooping something off a table.

Gift Giving. Exchanging gifts is important when doing business in India. Good choices are quality writing instruments (pens are status symbols in India), liquor (only if you know for sure the recipient drinks alcohol) and items your city, country or region is known for. As hostess gifts when invited to a person's home, imported cakes and chocolates are the best choices.

Avoid giving anything made of leather, which would offend the religious beliefs of Hindus. A U.S. once ambassador made the mistake of presenting Indian friends with photos set in leather frames, for example.

Presents should be carefully wrapped, using bright colors. Avoid white wrapping paper: white is the color of mourning. Use your right hand to present and accept gifts.

Wining and Dining. When entertaining Indian guests, remember that most Hindus are serious vegetarians. And because of the importance of family you can expect some of your guests to bring along some friends or relatives to your dinner. For these reasons buffet dinners are more practical. The buffet format not only provides flexible seating for unexpected guests, it also allows the food to be displayed on two tables at opposite ends of the room – one for vegetarians, the other for meat-eaters.

Speaking of meat, don't forget that Hindus (80 percent of the population) do not eat beef and that neither Muslims (12 percent) nor Hindus eat pork. Hindus of course revere the cow while both religious groups consider the pig unclean.

If you are a guest in a traditional Indian home, politely decline food or refreshments the first time they are offered. To accept immediately signifies greediness and poor breeding. By the same token, expect your Indian guests to similarly refuse. The gracious host or hostess responds by repeating the offer at least twice. It would be rude indeed to accept your guest's initial refusal at face value!

Further reading

Asia-Pacific Region and Global

Abegglen, James C. *Sea Change: Pacific Asia as the New World Industrial Center.* The Free Press, New York: 1994.

Axtell, Roger E. *Do's and Taboos Around the World.* John Wiley & Sons, 3rd ed. 1993.
Do's and Taboos of International Trade. Wiley, 2nd edition 1994.
Do's and Taboos of Hosting International Visitors. Wiley, 1990.
GESTURES: Do's and Taboo's of Body Language. Wiley, 1991.

Bartlett, Christopher A. and Ghoshal, Sumantra. *Managing Across Borders.* Harvard business School Press, Boston MA: 1998.

Brake, Walker and Walker. *Doing Business Internationally.* Irwin, New York: 1995.

De Vries, Mary A. *Internationally Yours.* Houghton Mifflin Co., New York: 1994.

Dunung, Sanjot P. *Doing Business in Asia.* Lexington Books, New York: 1995.

Foster, Dean Allen. *Bargaining Across Borders.* McGraw-Hill, New York: 1992.

Lasserre, Phillippe and Schütte, Helmut. *Strategies for Asia Pacific.* MacMillan Press, London: 1995.

Luo, Yadong. *Multinational Corporations in China.* Copenhagen Business School Press, Denmark: 2000.

Luo, Yadong. *China's Service Sector: A New Battlefield for International Corporations.* Copenhagen Business School Press, Denmark: 2001.

Kawatani, Takashi and Abdullah, Ahmad I. H. *Communication for Malaysian and Japanese Managers.* ISIS, Kuala Lumpur, Malaysia: 1996.

Morrison, Conaway, Borden. *Kiss, Bow or Shake Hands?* Adams Media Corp. (USA): 1994.

Morrison, Conaway, Douress. *Dun & Bradstreet's Guide to Doing Business Around the World.* Prentice Hall, New York: 1997.

Seitz, Konrad. China: *Eine Weltmacht kehrt Zurück.* Siedler Verlag,

Berlin (Verlagsgruppe Bertelsmann GmbH): 2000.

Zhan, James and Ozama, Terutomo. *Business Restructuring in Asia.* Copenhagen Business School Press, Denmark: 2001.

Japan

Clarke, Clifford H. and Lipp, Douglas G. *Danger and Opportunity: Resolving Conflict in U.S.-Based Japanese Subsidiaries.* Intercultural Press, Yarmouth, Maine: 1998.

DeMente, Boye. *How to Do Business with the Japanese.* NTC Business Books, Lincolnwood IL: 1993.

DeMente, Boye. *Japanese Etiquette and Ethics in Business.* NTL Business Books, Lincolnwood IL: 1994.

Hodgson, Day, Sano and Graham. *Doing Business with the New Japan.* Rowman and Littelfield, New York: 2000.

Johansson and Nonaka. *Relentless: The Japanese Way of Marketing.* Harper Business, New York: 1996.

Kato, Hiroki and Kato, Joan. *Understanding and Working with the Japanese Business World.* Prentice Hall, Englewood Cliff NJ: 1992.

Yamada, Haru. *Different Games, Different Rules: Why Americans and Japanese Misunderstand Each Other.* Oxford University Press, New York NY: 1997.

China

Bond, Michael Harris. *Beyond the Chinese Face: Insights from Psychology.* Oxford University Press, Hong Kong: 1991.

Chen, Ming-Jer. *Inside Chinese Business: A Guide to Managers Worldwide.* Harvard Business School Press, Boston MA: 2001.

Fang, Tony. *Chinese Business Negotiating Style.* Sage Publications, Thousand Oaks CA: 1999.

Hu and Grove. *Encountering the Chinese.* Intercultural Press, USA: 1991.

Kenna and Lacy. *Business China.* Passport Books, USA: 1994.

Seligman, Scott D. *Dealing with the Chinese.* Mercury Books, London: 1990.

Schneiter, Fred. *Getting Along with the Chinese.* Asia 2000 Ltd, Hong Kong: 1992.

Sinclair and Wong. *Culture Shock! China.* Times Books International, Singapore: 1990.

South Korea

DeMente, Boye. *Korean Etiquette and Ethics in Business.* NTC Business Books, Lincolnwood IL: 1994.

Hur and Hur. *Culture Shock! Korea.* Times Books International, Singapore: 1993.

Ungson, Steers and Park. *Korean Enterprise: The Quest for Globalization.* Harvard Business School Press, Boston MA: 1997.

Taiwan

Bates, Chris and Ling-li. *Culture Shock! Taiwan.* Graphic Arts, Portland OR: 1995.

Kenna, Peggy and Lacy, Sondra. *Business Taiwan.* Passport Books, USA: 1994.

The Philippines

Gochenour, Theodore. *Considering Filipinos.* Intercultural Press, USA: 1990.

Roces, Alfedo and Roces, Grace. *Culture Shock! Philippines.* Times Books International, Singapore: 1985.

Indonesia

Draine, Cathie and Hall, Barbara. *Culture Shock! Indonesia.* Times Books International, Singapore: 1986.

Malaysia

Datin Noor Aini Syed Amir. *Malaysian Customs and Etiquette.* Times Books, Singapore: 1991.

Munan, Heidi. *Culture Shock! Malaysia.* Times Books International, Singapore: 1991.

Thailand

Cooper, Nanthapa and Cooper, Robert. *Culture Shock! Thailand.* Times Books International, Singapore: 1982.

Cooper, Robert. *Thais Mean Business.* Times Books International, Singapore: 1995.

Holmes and Tangtontavy. *Working With The Thais.* White Lotus, Bangkok: 1995.

Vietnam

Ellis, Claire. *Culture Shock! Vietnam*. Times Books International, Singapore: 1995.

Jamieson, Neil. *Understanding Vietnam*. University of California Press, Berkeley CA: 1993.

Myanmar

Yin, Saw Myat. *Culture Shock! Burma*. Times Books International, Singapore: 1994.

India

Kolanad, Gitanjali. *Culture Shock! India*. Times Books International, Singapore: 1994.

Nepal

Burbank, Jon. *Culture Shock! Nepal*. Times Books International, Singapore: 1992.

Sri Lanka

Barlas and Wanasunder. *Culture Shock! Sri Lanka*. Times Books International, Singapore: 1992.

Pakistan

Mittman and Ihsan: *Culture Shock! Pakistan*. Times Books International, Singapore: 1991.